LEFT at the BIG WHITE PIG

A personal tale of heat monsters,
giant tortoises and
unexpected love

By Julia Tindall

ISBN:1478131756
ISBN-13: 978-1478131755

Dedicated to my dear friend Kat

We miss you….

We miss you...

CONTENTS

Part 4 And the fairy waved her magic wand…

Part 5 Galapagos

Afterthought

About Julia Tindall

ACKNOWLEDGMENTS

From my deepest heart, I would like to acknowledge all my teachers, past and present, especially the wonderful men who have peppered my personal story with such love, fun and grace.

Wiser beings than myself have shown up smack on time at crossroads on my journey to point me in the right direction. They have been angels in human form and I thank them profusely for the part they played in my personal life-movie.

I also want to thank my own guides and guardian angels from the spirit realms who have done such a magnificent job in arranging the right 'coincidences' to attract my attention when a life-change was necessary.

Most of all, I thank my dear friends, fellow yogis, jnana group practitioners and Sacramento community for playing and growing with me these past years and allowing me the space to fail and learn and grow, buoyed by their continued love and support.

Foreword

Dateline: March 18th 2012
Yelapa, Mexico

Most people look at my life and think it seems so darned perfect. I spend my time organizing yoga vacations and traveling to exotic locations around the world. In-between trips, I live in sunny Sacramento, California, and enjoy being the hub of a large community that loves and cares for each other.

I've just finished teaching my annual yoga retreat in Yelapa, Mexico, as much a paradise on earth as any I have encountered and am taking a couple of days to relax, rest and write. Beneath the open window of my small *palapa* overlooking the sea, fish are jumping, trying to escape the hungry tuna in the bay below, creating a sheen effect on the water. A florescent green hummingbird just appeared at the hibiscus bush, wings beating at lightening speed, sucking nectar out of the bright red flowers.

It feels appropriate to be writing this foreword here, because this place features strongly in my story, a story many people have asked me to write. In fact, this is where I turned left at the big white pig.

"How did a British woman like you end up living in Sacramento?" people would ask, "How did you get started leading yoga retreats?" "How can someone as wonderful as you still be single?" The questions have been at the volume of a dull roar.

More recently, after I turned fifty, I have also been asked, "How are you coping with aging?"

"Not well," was the answer that I frequently tried to

9

hide. I could still raise my energy enough to produce a great retreat, or teach a good yoga class, but the truth was I felt like I was declining; losing my looks; losing my power; losing my once legendary life force... was life going to be a slow downhill slide from now on?

In the past, I have resisted telling my tale. I don't consider myself a professional writer, even though I have had two self-help books published on the subject of *jnana* yoga (the yoga of self-inquiry); and the theme of an older woman facing a mid-life crisis who goes on a trip, finds change and begins a new life has been done, several times.

My own journey through this challenging period was the one that needed navigation. My compass was broken. The only way I could really see to fix it and still keep some kind of course of my own was to sit down and think through the life events that had brought me to this moment, remembering the wisdom I had learned along the way to see how that may serve me again now. This self-help woman needed help and it was clear that the help was inside myself. After all, the yoga of self-inquiry is my specialty. It was time to create a map of my life path that would help me regain my balance, my sense of wholeness, and my power as a woman.

Exactly a year ago, I began the self-reflection and inquiry that resulted in this book and my ultimate dream trip to the Galapagos Islands. I invite you on this particular journey with me. My hope is that during the course of our travels together over four continents and two decades, you will be inspired in your own lives, empowered and perhaps even entertained.

Julia Tindall

March 2012

Part 1

The Back Story

Chapter 1

Dateline: March 23rd, 2011
Sea of Cortez, Mexico

It all began with the sea lions. As our boat approached their colony in the Sea of Cortez, Mexico, the young ones jumped excitedly off the rocks and swam out to greet us, heads popping up out of the water to see who had come to play with them today. I donned wetsuit, snorkel and mask and jumped in. Holy schmolly! That water was cold enough to freeze the tail off a donkey! Heart beating rapidly but undeterred, I gamely swam towards one of the pups. He brushed past me, twirling and swirling around with grace and joy. Then another one joined us, actually nudging me with its nose, begging my participation in his aquatic antics.

I was having SUCH fun, until I saw a much bigger, no... make that enormous monster of a sea lion swim rapidly towards me, mouth open, teeth bared! You can't open your mouth and scream under water as your snorkel falls out of your mouth. Instead, adrenaline kicked in and I swam back to the boat as fast as I could, so as not to invade the big guy's territory any more than I had already. He didn't come after me, just swam away. But I had had my experience, and teeth chattering with cold, was happy to call it a day and climb back into the boat.

It was at that moment that I received the inspiration for this book. I cannot say it was necessarily the sea lions themselves that gave it to me. More likely it sprung from that intensely alive, joyful feeling that was like a life-blood coursing through my veins, a sense of can-do, anything is possible, it's never too late kind of feeling. The conversation I had had two nights ago under the stars with Mike and Alice came flooding back, crystal clear in my mind with the message attached... "Yes, you WILL go to Galapagos... and you will write about the experience... and discover more about who it is you are now as a fifty-something newly single woman with a still insatiable curiosity about the world.

****

Two days earlier, my friend Bob and I had arrived in Cabo San Lucas to start a weeklong vacation touring the Baja peninsula in Mexico. Bob is a retired engineer from Sacramento, my adopted hometown and has been a longtime yoga student and friend. Like me, he was getting fed-up with the unusually wet, cold weather we were having that spring and was anxious for some sunshine. He is easy-going and relaxed and I was delighted to have him as my traveling companion.

I had chosen to throw caution to the wind and rent a car and drive in Mexico for the first time. Bob was even more courageous for being my co-pilot and I had given him full permission to yell at me loudly if I failed to notice the odd goat, donkey or drunken caballero (Mexican cowboy) wandering into the road.

"We made it Bob, let's go!" I yelled as we fired up our little Chevy and drove out of the airport complex.

"Oh it feels so good to be warm again," exclaimed Bob, as he peeled off his winter sweater and threw it in the back seat, stretching his legs out with a sigh of satisfaction. I wound the windows down and felt the warm breeze caress my hair, blowing away some of the stresses and concerns of the last few weeks. As we hit the main road for Cabo San Lucas, I could feel the tension in my knotted forehead start to relax.

For the past twenty years, I have been a yoga instructor based in Sacramento, California and lead yoga retreats locally and around the world. It's a wonderful way of life, but comes with no regular paycheck, no assurances of bills paid or money left over each month for luxuries. I love my work, as it is my passion, but being self-employed means cultivating a relationship with economic uncertainty. As someone who tends to worry and with marketing and event planning details filling my head, I don't always manage to stay stress-free.

The last few weeks at home had been particularly exhausting for me. I had been offering a lot of groups and workshops recently and when I teach, I give it my all, my full Presence and energy. It is my joy to do so and although I feel very blessed by the work I have chosen, I can also get very tired. I HAVE to take care of myself and have found that getting completely away out of town is the best way for me to relax. I also feel that that is a responsibility to my students. They want the best Julia possible to show up as their guide and mentor and I need to make sure that happens.

We drove on for a while in a shared silence of contentment.

Then Bob turned to me and said, "Julia, you've seemed a bit on edge recently. What's been going on with you?"

He was right. In addition to the day-to-day stresses of life, I was not feeling like my old self. Since turning fifty, I was having a really hard time dealing with menopause symptoms.

"You know, Bob, I'm not sleeping well and feel so tired all the time. Lack of sleep makes me feel shaky and weak. I'm not always thinking clearly. To be honest, I'm really fed up with it and am hoping this vacation will help me feel better."

"Not sleeping is hard! Well hopefully the sunshine and all the fresh air will help," offered Bob sweetly.

"Yes and at least I am doing something I really want to do! I can't wait to swim with those sea-lions!"

Swimming with sea lions was something I had put on my bucket list recently during one of my *jnana* yoga groups; it's a list of things I wanted to experience before I "kicked the bucket!" I run a *jnana* yoga group every

14

Tuesday in my house in Sacramento. *Jnana* means wisdom. It's yoga for the mind, not the body. We use yogic tools and practices to watch our egos in action and empower ourselves to bring more consciousness into our daily lives. It's a place of non-judgment where everyone feels free to share what is in their hearts and minds, a weekly touchstone of sanity and peace in an often insane world.

As one of our group practices a few months ago, we had all written out our bucket lists. It was a powerful practice for me, as it showed me clearly where my desires lay and started me thinking about how I was going to manifest them. For example, when I read a blog about a friend of mine swimming with sea lions in La Paz, Mexico, it gave me the idea to go on this particular trip.

A trip to Galapagos was also on that list, but at that time, it had felt out of reach, too expensive for my yoga teacher's budget. I had put that desire on the back burner.

The impetus to offer a class on writing bucket lists had come after my fiftieth birthday rolled around. Turning fifty had actually been a bit of a shock to my system. For a start, it sounds old. I guess it's because when I was young, people who were fifty looked and acted way older than our generation does now and as a healthy, young-looking and acting person, it was hard for me to think of myself in that category. I did, at least, have an awesome celebration to welcome in this sixth decade of life. I teach a yoga retreat every summer at a magical place in the mountains near Tahoe called Sierra Hot Springs. Nestled in a lovely valley with cows grazing in the meadow, the main house is a cozy Victorian with big fireplaces, friendly cats and a plush green-carpeted workshop space that you can rent. Outside in the woods are the hot springs themselves, deliciously warm, sulphur-laden waters that caress and soothe the body with their healing mineral content.

I had rented the space for the whole weekend and invited thirty-five of my friends to come up and play. They told me, "Julia, you are not to do a thing! We will organize classes for the group and provide entertainment and cake!"

We all enjoyed a beautiful weekend of yoga, an amazing breath-work session, a cabaret and dancing.

Then I went home.

And had a mid-life crisis.

It suddenly hit me hard that I now had less of life left to live than had already been lived.

How did this happen? How did time fly by so fast that I am half way though this lifespan already? And for sure the last few years it has sped up. I researched this particular perception and found out that there is, in fact, some truth as to why this is a common experience. It's apparently to do with the ratio of time experienced by the mind and time passing. For a five year old who has just had a birthday, waiting for the next one to roll around seems like an eternity as it represents a sixth of her life so far. But for a fifty year old, next year is a smaller percentage of life experienced to date, so appears to go quicker. So time feels like it's moving faster. Great. And it will continue to speed up.

Oh boy.

Then a few weeks later, menopause hit me like a ton of bricks.

Up till then I had been lucky. I may have been fifty, but still had very few lines on my face. My muscles were strong and toned from lots of yoga, and I had very few "feminine problems" that often plague other women like monthly mood swings or cramps.

But one night, literally overnight, that all changed. I lay down in bed to go to sleep and the heat monster came. What the hell? It was a cool, winter's night and suddenly it felt like I was sitting in a sauna!

At first it was a little scary. Was I sick? Did I have a temperature? I didn't feel unwell... I just lay there, kicked the covers off and sweated for a while, and as quickly as it had come, the heat went away. I soon began to feel cold again. I pulled the covers back over me and went to sleep, only to be awoken shortly afterwards with another visit from the heat monster! Covers off again, sweating.

It dawned on me this was a hot flash. I was not immune after all. YIKES!! I eventually dropped off to sleep but woke up about four times more during the night sweating and hot. Covers off, then five minutes later, covers on again. Why hadn't somebody warned me? I had vaguely heard rumors about menopausal symptoms but it seemed like no big deal the way it was whispered around. How are we women supposed to sleep with the heat monster attacking us every few minutes?

I remember so clearly getting up the next morning tired and perplexed about these changes in my body and noticing with horror that my face had dropped half an inch overnight. A line had appeared on my lower cheek where previously there had been none and there was some loose hanging flesh around my chin. "Good God! I'm looking like an old lady!" I wailed to myself. And what were those dark hairs doing above my mouth? I'd never noticed them before, but on closer examination, yes, it was true, I was growing a moustache!

I sank down on the couch and for the first time in my life, felt depressed. Here I was, fifty-something, hormones changing, periods stopped, done as a potential Mother, options diminishing as a potential lover and darn it all, I suddenly could not remember what was even on my schedule for the day. My mind had gone blank. But MY mind NEVER goes blank! What was happening to me? Was I getting dementia already? I felt a shudder of fear course through my body. Oh God, have I done what I came to this earth to do yet? What if I don't? What if I run out of time or energy? Panic started to set in... what AM I meant to do in this now terribly short seeming life span anyway?

Now I have to let you into a little secret here. I do have great faith in the invisible realms. How that translates for me is that I speak to my spirit guides and guardian angels whenever I feel I need some help. I am not a particularly psychic person. I don't see them or hear voices, yet I feel that I do receive guidance and know that it must come from somewhere. I have been known to yell loudly at them with passion and verve. This was one of those times. Still sitting on the couch, I screamed out, "Tell me what I'm meant to do! Is this it or is there more?"

I asked inwardly, waiting for a message to pop into my head; I took a couple of deep breaths and then I heard, like a whisper in my mind, *"Relax. It will all unfold."*

"That's all very well for you to say," I yelled at my invisible guides. "You aren't over half-way through your life span and slowly turning into a man!"

Silence; just the echo of my thoughts and the sound of my heart beating faster. It was one of those "well, maybe it will never happen to me" scenarios where I had never given menopause any thought because no one really talked about it and I had only vaguely heard murmurings about the symptoms. So I did what pretty much every woman does in a moment of high anxiety – I ate a chocolate bar and called my girlfriends.

First, I called my friend Judith, who is a few years older than me.
"Hi Judith", "it's Julia. Do you have a minute?"

"Sure," said Judith, "what's up?"

"I think I've entered menopause. I was up a lot of the night sweating, so I wanted to know how it's been for you and how you deal with it. Any advice?"

Now Judith is a wise soul, a shaman and a healer and if anyone would know how to deal with this, she would.

"I've been going through this for ten years already and I can tell you that the heat comes and goes. Sometimes it is quite annoying and I wake up with the sheets soaked. Other times it will go away for months. But that's not the worst of it... the vagina also gets really dry and it can be painful to have sex."

"WHAT!!!" I screamed inwardly! "Ten years of sweat, no sleep and agonizing sex? You have to be kidding! How do women deal with this?"

I regained my composure and calmly said, "So what have you done about it? Has anything helped you?"

" I put on wild yam cream to balance my hormones but other than that, just bring a little fan with me in my purse in case I get a flash to help stay cool."

"Thanks, Judith. I'll look into that cream," I muttered, somewhat unconvinced.

Next I called Sally. Her advice was to sleep under a fan, the kind you can pull on with a long cord from your bed when you wake up hot so you don't have to get out of bed to switch it on, thereby waking yourself up more fully and having an even harder time getting back to sleep. She had been getting visits from the heat monster for six years already and is my age. Maybe I am actually lucky to be fifty and only now experiencing "the change."

I called my Mother in England. She reminded me that she had had a hysterectomy and the doctors had put her straight on HRT, hormone replacement therapy, but that had resulted in her developing ovarian cancer years later. Obviously not an option for me!

I felt as though I was at the mercy of unstoppable forces and needed something to cheer me up. A trip to Mexico would be just the ticket.

I had also just broken up with Ken, the man I had been involved with for the past few years. The emotional stress of that was weighing heavily on me, as he was a loving, wonderful man and many people would think me crazy to break if off with him. But my soul was screaming out for space, for more time alone. This match had somehow been just not quite right. If I wanted "the right one" then I HAD to let go of the "not-quite-right-one".

In the past, I had gone through periods when being single felt like a desperate, lonely place, but this time, I was not afraid of being alone. In fact, I welcomed it. Like Madonna, who is coincidentally about my age, I felt the need to reinvent myself now that I was in my fifties. I needed to press the pause button and take a break from men, from my daily routines and my career. I wanted the clarity that comes from distancing myself from day-to-day life and having time away would give me the space I needed to do just that.

As it turned out, the timing for this much-needed trip to Baja was perfect. Bob was able to join me, my schedule opened up and rain was forecast for the Sacramento region that week.

Landing in Mexico had brought back memories, too, reminding me of a time in my life many years ago when I had let go of the relationship I'd had during my twenties, ditched a dream job in London and spent a year backpacking around the USA and Mexico, where my life took an unexpected U-turn.

Here I was again, creating time and space in my life for something new to come in, open for inspiration, guidance and healing.

Sometimes, though, we need to look back in order to move forwards....

Chapter 2

Dateline: March 23rd, 2011
Baja California

The afternoon sun was shining brightly as we gaily navigated our way through the tourist traps of Los Cabos and headed north to the magical, artsy town of Todos Santos to track down our first night's accommodations. When I travel, my preference is to seek out interesting, unique places to stay. I had found 'The Surf Shack' on the Internet and the website promised great views, tranquility and the sound of the waves to lull us to sleep; and for under $100 a night, the price was right too. After a couple of hours driving, we saw the sign for 'The Surf Shack' from the main road and turned left down a dusty track feeling optimistic.

"If we are lucky, we'll just make it for sunset!" I suggested. Then "*pow*", we hit a pothole and the car bounced a foot into the air. "Hey, mind my butt," said Bob good-naturedly! We came to a fork in the track. No signs, no one to ask..."What do you think, Bob? Left or right?"

"Let's try right, and see where we end up."

Five minutes later, the track turned onto a cliff-frontage road. I'm being generous with the word road... it was still a rutted, sandy track, but at least we now saw some buildings up ahead that looked well-cared for and populated. Shortly after, we saw a big sign proclaiming our arrival the 'The Surf Shack'. We had just made sunset and excitedly ran out towards the beach to catch a last glimpse of the setting sun over the Pacific Ocean before finding our host, Matt and checking in.

"Look, Bob, it's absolutely gorgeous!" I proclaimed happily, taking in the panorama before my eyes - a long,

long strip of sand, absolutely deserted and peppered only sporadically with the odd house on the cliff top. Pelicans still dived for a last evening meal before turning in to wherever pelicans spend the night. (Where DO pelicans spend the night?) It looked untouched and timeless from our cliff-top hideaway and I couldn't wait to explore more.

Meanwhile we were starving hungry! Matt, Our friendly Canadian host gave us a restaurant recommendation in Todos Santos and we hopped back in the car to wind our way through the sandy maze once again, to the main road.

Todos Santos is an old town famous for its art galleries, boutique hotels and glorious restaurants. It's quickly becoming a favorite for ex-pats and snowbirds and has undergone a rapid transformation in recent years as more and more of the lovely, old buildings downtown have been renovated and re-invented. We headed to The Hotel California. Was it THE Hotel California from the Eagles' Song? Well – it is on a dark, desert highway, in Mexico... in my imagination this must have been the place. And the romance of it did not disappoint. If you happen to like cobbled stone entranceways, antique furnishings and crumbling red brick exteriors as I do, then this would be your cup of tea. Plus their new Mexican gourmet restaurant had just opened that week!

"There's a table for us over in the corner, Bob, look," I said as we walked into the charming dining room!" We got seated and proceeded to the next item of business – a drink! After a long day traveling, a cocktail to welcome us to our vacation was just the ticket. As we were ordering a margarita, the Belgian chef came out to chat to us.

"I recommend the tuna," he said. "Fresh caught just a few hours ago and seared lightly in my secret sauce. And as you are among our first guests, I will give you some Belgian chocolates to try as my gift to you after dinner."

Oh I had died and gone to heaven.... fabulous food, drink, ambience and chocolates too! What a great way to start our week! It was all delicious and we ate our fill. With satisfied bellies, we headed back to the dusty track and our cliff-top shack.

Shack is perhaps a rather unfair description of our lodging. Matt the owner, a surfer, had built these apartments in a rather hodge-podge but nevertheless interesting style, each one being different and separated by a lovely cactus garden interspersed with hammocks and lounge chairs. They were simply yet comfortably furnished and ours had two bedrooms and a kitchen. We arrived home as the night was starting to cool, grabbed a sweater and headed to the beach for some serious stargazing.

Ahh – desert skies... so clear, so star-studded. "Look, Julia," said Bob, "is that a bonfire down the beach?" A few yards away we could see what looked like a small fire outside one of the other houses. I guess it's a tribal thing, but I am always drawn to campfires. We wandered over. There was no one there but it somehow felt OK just to sit down next to the fire and enjoy it.

Before too long a man came out. "I immediately jumped up and apologized. "Hello. I hope you don't mind, we saw the fire and it looked so inviting. We very rudely just sat down!"

"No that's fine. You are more than welcome to join us. My name's Alan, by the way."

"I'm Julia and this is my friend Bob."

"Nice to meet you. And where are you guys from?"

"From Sacramento, California. We just arrived today. How about you?"

"We are all from Vancouver. Actually I live here and care-take the houses here on the cliff. My brother Mike is renting this one with his wife, Alice. Oh here they are... hey Mike – bring a couple of glasses out for our new friends."

Mike appeared with a bottle of wine and glasses for us.

"Wow thanks!" I said, immediately cementing my opinion about the amazing hospitality of Canadians.

Alan stoked the fire as we huddled round, warming ourselves against the rapidly dropping desert temperatures. We shared the usual traveler formalities of how long have you been here, where have you been, where are you going, and discovered that Mike and Alice had just spent a few months touring South America. My attention perked up. I have spent many years traveling the globe, often alone when I was younger and for months at a time. But this was one continent I had not yet explored thoroughly.

"So what was the highlight for you?" I asked, with a very real curiosity.

"The Galapagos Islands in Ecuador," said Alice, "without a doubt. It is one of the most magical places on the planet and still so pristine. The wildlife experiences are phenomenal. We saw the giant tortoises, blue-footed boobies and huge iguanas. They were so tame. If we weren't careful, we would trip over them!"

"Isn't that where Charles Darwin wrote his theory of evolution?" asked Bob.

"Yes," replied Alice. "His observation of the slight variations in the birds of different islands prompted the whole theory and turned the world of the Creationists upside down back in the nineteenth century."

"Oh I SO want to go there," I said, "But all the cruises round the islands I have seen are way out of my price range. They seem to run at least $3,500 for the week."

"Not at all," Mike chimed in. "You can get last minute deals for way less than that and if you go as an independent traveler and hang out on the beaches you will meet fishermen who will take you around at a fraction of the usual cost. We stayed a few weeks and just loved it."

Do you know when the Divine is trying to tell you something? For me it's when I get a tingly feeling up my spine, a sense of 'yes', an excitement in my body that gets me feeling high… and I was having that feeling right then.

"OK", I thought. "I could go to Galapagos, especially if I travel the way I used to when I was younger, as an independent traveler with no fixed agenda, just a map and a guidebook. If I go this time next year, that would give me twelve whole months to organize my finances and my schedule. I would also need to be feeling fit and energetic to make this trip - what an incentive to figure out what to do about my hormones and get my body back in balance!"

****

The next day, Bob and I walked down the long, deserted beach to find a breakfast spot. We ended up at a brand new posh Eco-lodge which served to-die-for coffee and killer omelets. The sky was a never-ending Baja blue and the sun felt comfortably warm on my skin. One of the practices I had learned as a tantra teacher was to become aware of the senses as I go through my day, and here my senses were on high alert; taste buds rejoicing, the smell of the coffee, feel of the sunlight, sound of the waves. I could feel the tensions of the last few weeks melting away as I relaxed deeper into the precious moment and all it offered. I took a deep breath in and slowly exhaled, feeling so grateful for having the ability to be in this special place, far from crowds. I live in a city and although my house is quiet, there is always that background hum of traffic and city noise, that energy of activity that permeates even my peaceful oasis.

But here there was just the ocean, the desert and the endless sky. My nervous system could let go of its defenses and relax deeply. Isn't this why we take vacations, to truly get recharged and let go of our stress? Yet so many people opt to go to high octane, busy destinations that in their way encourage even more stimulation and stress; not my cup of tea if I have come to relax. I need the soothing sounds of nature. This beach at Pescadero, just south of Todos Santos suited me just fine.

But Bob and I had a big agenda for our week and had more places to visit. We headed to La Paz next, enjoying a kayak trip across the bay and swimming with the sea lions, where I got the inspiration to write this book. From there, we headed south through lovely oasis-style desert towns to the undiscovered coral reef area of Cabo Pulmo. We took another boat trip to snorkel the reef, once more enduring freezing cold water in our efforts to admire the fragile reef system of corals and colorful fish. Who knew the water in Baja could be that cold? Certainly not me! Now I know why everyone stays poolside.

As our week drew to a close, we headed back south to Cabo San Lucas for our last night in Mexico, staying in a small hotel right in the middle of the old town, where all the famous restaurants and bars are located.

After dinner that last evening, Bob invited me to choose a place for dessert. Always one to seek out the perfect *flan*, the Mexican version of crème caramel, I decided on Sammy Hagar's Cabo Wabo restaurant as *flan* was on the menu. I didn't recognize the place. I had been there twenty-two years earlier on my first trip to Baja and it looked very different. We ordered the *flan*.

Oh my God – the search was over! This was hands-down THE best *flan* I had ever eaten in my life! Smooth, incredibly creamy, melt-in-your mouth custard with a decadent caramel sauce that had just the right balance of sweetness and flavor. Well worth the $10 tab; in fact, worth a visit to Cabo just to sample!

Feeling satisfied and content and with memory banks stimulated, I turned to Bob and said, "Did you know that this place was actually where my life took a U-turn twenty-some years ago?"

"No", said Bob, "How was that?"

"Let's order another couple of *flans* and I will tell you the story."

Chapter 3

Dateline: January 1988
Cabo San Lucas

A month ago, I had left a dream job working as an advertising executive for Nature magazine in London and decided to spend a year traveling around the American continent. Life in London no longer appealed to me. I had seen every West End show, eaten at many fine restaurants and explored much of Europe. But something in my soul was crying out for a change. So I resigned from my job, took my savings and trusty red backpack and flew west to California.

After visiting with my girlfriend, Shelley, in San Diego, she kindly drove me to Ensenada, Mexico to continue my journey. I would say at that time I was very content to be in my own company and quite okay about traveling alone. A beach, a good book, a glass of vino and I was a happy camper. I spoke reasonable Spanish so I had no fear of being in Mexico alone, in fact, I relished the prospect of brushing up my language skills. I was of average height, athletic build and had long, messy blonde hair that I used to tie up in a ponytail when it was too hot on my neck. I was bold, determined and brash, with an out-going personality and a thirst for adventure. Completely carefree, I had no fear and no real plan, just a vague notion of exploring Mexico for the next few months.

I took the bus through Baja all the way to Cabo san Lucas. It took twenty-four hours and was one of those bus-rides from hell you swear you will never repeat. Still, I was hardy and resilient, and enjoyed the never-ending scenery of cactus, cactus and more cacti, such a contrast from green old England.

Arriving in Cabo, I found a small, cheap hotel in the center of town and after a meal of enchiladas and red wine, decided to wander around the town. It was quite small and friendly in those days, with not so many choices of places to go. Cabo Wabo was THE watering hole in town and full of fishermen, boating types and the odd scruffy backpacker like me. I bought a drink and stayed for a while, people-watching, and when tiredness set in after my long journey, left to go back to the hotel.

Unbeknown to me, in that same bar sat Kathy and Kevin, bored out of their skulls and totally not digging the rowdy drinking vibe. Kathy turned to Kevin and said, "Who do you think is the most interesting person in the bar?" Kevin looked around and pointed towards me. "That blonde over there. There's something about her."

And that was it. End of conversation, they told me afterwards. But my presence had been duly noted.

The next day, I walked towards the ferry for the mainland, bought a ticket and got in line for the boat.

I just happened to be standing in the queue behind Kathy and Kevin! Kathy turned around; "Hello, didn't I see you in Cabo Wabo last night?" she asked with a friendly smile.

"Yes," I said, "I stopped by for a drink, but didn't stay long. It's really not my scene. Too many crazy drunks for my taste and as I was on my own, I felt a bit uncomfortable."

"I'm not surprised," said Kevin. " We felt the same way. Still they do make a great margarita!"

"Where are you headed?" I asked.

"Puerto Vallarta," replied Kevin. "We've got ten days left of our vacation and thought we'd go check it out. After that we're not sure."

"Oh me too!" How fun, I thought. I may have just found me some traveling companions.

A few minutes into our getting to know you chitchat, a lovely young African American girl approached us. "Mia, meet Julia. She's going to PV too. Maybe we can all hang out together."

We sat on the boat deck, Julia, Mia, Kathy and Kevin, and talked and talked and talked. It turned out we had a lot in common. Kathy and Kevin were Bikram yoga teachers. They had been amongst the first students to take what was then a fairly new form of hatha yoga, created by Bikram Choudry, which was becoming popular with Hollywood celebrities. They lived in Ashland, Oregon and had a small yoga studio there. Kevin was of slight build, with longish hair that made him look quite the hippy. He had a sensitive, insightful way about him and I could soon tell he was a person of depth and strength. Kathy was slim with brown, curly hair and a charming smile. She was the chattier one of the couple and she and I hit it off like a house-on-fire. Mia was a tall, willowy beauty from San Diego and had just spent a few weeks on a sailing boat that had finally docked in Cabo. She was still a student and was taking some time off between studies. She had the most infectious laugh and soon had us smiling with her.

We reached the mainland of Mexico and took a rickety old bus down to Puerto Vallarta (PV). The bus station was located in the lovely old part of town complete with whitewashed houses and cobbled streets lined with food vendors and sombrero sellers. We were all traveling on a budget and cheap was key, so we decided to all share a room and managed to find a run-down old hotel in the old town with four beds at a rock-bottom price.

I was immediately charmed by PV; this was the Mexico I had dreamed of! That evening, as we walked the *Molecon*, the Promenade that goes the length of the sea-front, I felt a sense of euphoria. It was January, the weather was warm, I had newfound friends, and a sense of infinite possibility. The local people were out in force too, buying strawberries in little plastic cups from the street vendors, and long doughnutty snacks covered in powdered sugar.

I found out that this was the town that had been made famous by Elizabeth Taylor and Richard Burton when he and Ava Gardner were here filming "Night of the Iguana"

29

back in the 1950s. He and Liz had just started their romance and the worlds' press descended on this sleepy Mexican town, which attracted huge amounts of attention to the area and prompted a boost in investment and tourism, which has continued unabated to this day.

The following morning we got up to hunt down the fresh-squeezed orange juice man and started our day with a healthy juice and *huevos rancheros,* eggs in a tomato-based sauce. We explored the local markets selling Mexican lace, maracas and intricate Huichol Indian beaded trinkets. I've never been a big shopper and had very little room in my backpack for purchases, but enjoyed practicing my high-school Spanish with the locals and admiring the art that was for sale.

The highlight of the day was seeing a whale and her calf playing in the Bay! She came within a few feet of shore and jumped and twirled as if to put on a show for the picture-snapping tourists! I had never seen a whale before and had no idea they came to the Bay of Banderas to calf and nurse. It was thrilling for me to see a wildlife show so unexpectedly. Maybe this was a good omen for things to come.

After the excitement of the whale show, we wandered further down the beach and were accosted by a man selling boat tickets.

"Come to Yelapa!" he shouted. "Only $5 on the Princess Yelapa; leaves tomorrow morning at 9:00 a.m. You like VERY much. Eat pie with the pie ladies and see waterfall – very beautiful."

"Let's go," said Kevin. "I've heard Yelapa is a really cool place. Besides. It's just a day trip."

Or so we thought.

Quite honestly, I probably would not have gone there at all without Kevin's urging. It's funny to look back and see how certain people come into our lives as little angels, prompting us to make the moves that need to happen for our destiny to unfold. Kevin was one such angel for me.

30

But at that time I was innocent of my future and was simply happy to be carried along on this blissful wave of fun and friendship.

So the next morning, daypacks stuffed with water, sun-cream, towels and camera, we boarded the Princess Yelapa for the two-hour cruise through the Bay. What a beautiful Bay it was! We left the built-up area of hotels and condos and started heading west along the coast, coming across an area of big rocky protrusions, one with a giant natural arch, where snorkelers were checking out the abundant sea-life under water.

The sun was shining brightly and flying fish skipped above the waves, escaping some unknown predator. The further west we went, the more any sign of civilization disappeared until all we could see were steep, jungle-covered cliffs descending abruptly into the ocean, not a soul in sight. We passed a couple of pretty, deserted beaches and one or two fishermen in small *pangas* (boats) looking for the day's catch. The four of us relaxed on deck, enjoying each other's company, the warm, winter sunshine and pleasant ocean breezes.

Then the boat suddenly turned a corner and we saw in front of us the most beautiful bay I have ever seen in my life.... a perfect curved, sandy beach lined with picturesque palm trees and little *palapa* huts that looked like they had been lifted from the *South Pacific* set! On one side of the bay was a small, fishing village and above it, scattered amongst the trees, I could make out a few houses. No cars, no roads. It looked idyllic and I felt my heart skip a beat and leap with excitement at the possibility of spending a day exploring this tropical paradise.

We unloaded from the larger vessel onto smaller fishing boats that could take us through the surf to land on the beach and we were greeted by a gaggle of kids all shouting at once.

"I have *burro* for you – take you to waterfall – very nice."

"My auntie is Carmen the Pie Lady – she has best pies

31

in Yelapa!"

"Come to Carlos' restaurant, freshest fish on the beach!"

Well after our voyage, the pie sounded good so we allowed ourselves to be led to Carmen, the pie lady with the best pies, to see what she had. I was amazed! Someone had taught these Mexican ladies to make the most delicious pies you can imagine! Coconut cream, chocolate pie, lemon meringue, pecan, banana cream...we each chose a different one so we could taste them all and agreed they were yummy!

With pie-fueled bellies, we decided to explore first and eat lunch later, so we headed across the beach towards the fishing village where we heard the waterfall was located. Behind the beach is a lagoon formed by a river that empties out to the sea right under the cliff. The lagoon is home to a large variety of exotic-looking birds that I had never seen before. Large, white cranes, black cormorants, small, delicate looking wading birds and of course, the ubiquitous pelican. We could see the river stretching back into the jungly hinterland, beckoning more exploration, but we were on a quest for that waterfall.

After wading through the river, which cuts into the beach before meeting the ocean, we saw a cliff looming ahead. A hand-written sign said *TO VILLAGE* and an arrow pointed up some rough-hewn steps cut into the cliff that looked like they led right into someone's back yard! Well, they did, actually. We dodged the washing line with *pantalones* flapping in the breeze and climbed upwards behind the houses, eventually finding a dusty trail that led to the village.

A local man on a donkey rode by at a trot. We stopped to let them pass and as I turned around, I almost gasped... the view across the bay and beach was unbelievably gorgeous! Photo time, for sure. I did not want to forget this in a hurry! A pig and her piglets ambled towards us as we navigated the narrow, dusty lane down towards the village. We crossed a bridge over a little creek and saw an adorable little church up ahead. Although many remote Mexican villages still have their traditional Indian beliefs, most of them are now fully converted to Catholicism and Yelapa was no exception. The church was eerily quiet, with a simple beauty and a peaceful energy acquired from decades of devotion. We stopped to rest and I remember giving thanks for the opportunity to be there and for all the blessings I had received so far on this trip. I am not a religious person, but I do believe strongly in taking time to practice gratitude as much as possible and just being in a church is, for me, a good reminder to do just that.

Kevin was already outside when I came out, looking intently at the ground.

"If we just follow the donkey poop, I bet it will lead us to the waterfall," he said with a grin. He was right. The donkey poop left a clearly marked trail that helped lead us through the maze of the village paths up to the waterfall trail. As we climbed higher, the path got narrower and the river noise louder. After about ten minutes, the trail ended in a clump of rocks. We scrambled over them and saw in front of us a lovely ribbon of water cascading down from a jungle cliff. We were hot after the walk and jumped into the pool below the waterfall, screeching like little kids.

"This is AWESOME!" I yelled.

"I LOVE it here!" Kathy responded.

There was a local man sitting next to the pool selling cold drinks and orange juice. How convenient! We indulged in a fresh juice and settled on some rocks to dry off. While we were there, an American lady came to swim too. Kevin started chatting with her and found out she was renting a house in Yelapa for a month and absolutely loved it! She told us there were lots of houses for rent and many gringos came for the winter season.

"There is a special vibration in this place. Can you feel it?" asked Kevin. "I think we should stay here. Let's go and take a look at some houses for rent and see what we find."

I didn't feel a thing but did agree that this was an amazing place, so I went along with the others. The

American lady had told us that if we asked around in the village, someone would be sure to have something to suit us.

She was right. In the local market, Ana told us she had a house to rent big enough for four and "would we please see." We followed her around the dusty town, then up into the hills for about five minutes along a narrow trail and came across a tumbledown shack that she proudly presented as her rental house. Inside was filthy with dust and dirt; insects crawled around, the kitchen was unusable and the bathroom was a hole in the ground outside; no shower; three mangy-looking beds with no sheets, holey mosquito nets and grungy mattresses.

"We'll take it!" exclaimed Kevin!

I looked at him with horror... I mean at that time I wasn't that fussy about where I stayed, but this place was a filthy dump! Besides, I am terrified of spiders!

"It will be fine for a few days," said Kathy. We can go back on the *Princess Yelapa* and get our bags then come back the next day and be here for the rest of our trip." (They had another week left of vacation.) Mia agreed that was a good plan, so we set off back to the beach for a fish lunch before heading back to PV to grab our stuff.

I must say, our basic hotel in the town seemed like a paradise compared to the *palapa* in Yelapa. I was really not enthusiastic about this move, but was so enjoying being with my friends, I was willing to try this jungle experience so I could be with them as long as possible. After all, if it was really awful, I could always move on alone.

So the next day, having stocked up on toilet paper and insect repellent, we caught the local water taxi back to Yelapa and settled in to our new abode. Despite my misgivings, tiredness won out and somehow I made it through the night in our shack.

We spent the following day discovering more about this enchanting place.

Down at the beach, we started to meet people. It soon

became obvious that there was one beach restaurant that catered to the "local gringos" while the rest serviced the day-tripping tourists. We soon settled in and got to know many of the North Americans who lived down here for much of the year.

There was Linda, a lady in her fifties who had a lovely *palapa* in the hills where she taught kundalini yoga classes; Lang, an affable trust-fund baby with a big house that sported amazing views across the bay and had one of the only two hot showers in Yelapa at that time; Miki Shapiro, wife of a late Hollywood record producer who had invited Bob Dylan, Donovan and other notables to stay at their palatial home right behind the beach back in the sixties; and Isabel, queen of the Point area, the left-hand side of the bay, where she tended her lovely garden and a charming collection of *palapas* that she rented out by the month. These were much nicer than the one we had found; pricier too, but still a great deal compared with the USA.

Mani, a larger-then-life white-haired timeshare salesman was taking a break from his job and commanded the beach party with his vibrant personality and joking ways.

"Come up to my place out on the Point any time you like," he said. "It's really quiet up there with just the sound of the waves. I have a hammock under the porch that is the perfect place to read a book and lots of books on the shelf. You can help yourself."

To our delight, we found there was a dance at the Yacht Club every Wednesday and Saturday. 'Yacht Club' conjured up an image of posh yachting types sipping cocktails on a terrace overlooking their luxury yachts. Nothing could have been further from the truth! It turned out that the Yacht Club was purely the local name for a gringo-run Mexican restaurant where the tables were cleared away after dinner to make room for a good old-fashioned disco! It was hippy heaven! Dancing away to new sounds, oldies, Mexican beat and rock and roll, we all mashed together under the stars overlooking the small fishing village beach, boogying the night away to our heart's content.

The following day was a full moon and on every full moon there is a beach party and bonfire on the beach (still is today). Someone had a guitar and we sat around singing and enjoying the vibe with a bunch of others, old and young, it didn't matter; we all enjoyed the scene together. I have always fancied myself as a bit of a singer, so I grabbed a guitar and started to play a rousing rendition of "The Night they Drove Old Dixie Down." When I had finished, the guy sitting next to me said, "I wrote that song!" I had no idea who he was. I was only familiar with the Joan Baez version and had never heard of a group called "The Band" who had written and recorded it first. I was duly unimpressed and could not tell you what he even looked like. It was dark. But it turned out I had unwittingly bumped into a rock legend and had unceremoniously murdered his song right in front of him!

A few days later, Kathy, Kevin and Mia had to head for home. I had had enough of the filthy shack and had discovered by then that Isabel up on the Point had couch space she rented for cheap, so I moved myself up to her main house. It was clean, communal and being up on the hill had great views over the ocean.

Being out on the Point area at the end of the Bay, I decided to take Mani up on his offer to visit his place, and walked further down the trail to find his *palapa*. He was not home, but no one locks doors in Yelapa. I walked in to find myself alone with an old shaggy dog and looked around. The house was neat and tidy, and right outside I spied the hammock under the hanging basket of flowers. It did look inviting. I looked at the books on the shelf and saw a big blue volume called "A Course in Miracles." Intrigued, I pulled it down and settled in the hammock to read.

I will never forget what happened next. I opened to the first page, which said,

"This is A Course in Miracles. This is a required course. Only the time you take it is voluntary. Free will does not mean that you can establish the curriculum. It means only that you can elect what you want to take at a given time."

As the Truth of those words seeped into my being and reached deep into my heart, I burst into tears. I had no idea why. It was as though some Divine force was bathing me in the sweetest love imaginable and all I could do was say "yes" to it and open my heart to receive. What power was in those pages and why did it have that effect on me? I had never been one to cry easily. As a stoic Brit, I had always been guarded about showing my feelings and had learned the art of numbing out at an early age, tending to retreat to the familiar safety of my head if things got uncomfortable.

But this was different. It felt like a homecoming, a set-up that had been waiting for exactly that moment, this place and those words to line up together and create this expansive opening inside me. Although I would return on subsequent days to read more and discover how the book got channeled through a reluctant, scientifically-inclined atheist a few years ago, on that day I just stayed with the first page and allowed the tears to roll.

We all have defining moments in life when something cracks us open and changes us for good, and this was one for me. I walked slowly back along the coastal path towards the village that day slower, softer, more open than before. My conscious, unmistakable relationship with the Divine had begun. Looking back, it had always been there; during the times I had hitch-hiked through Southern Africa as a teen, yet felt somehow invincible and protected, despite the obvious danger; the guidance that helped me so easily get that dream job in London, the only one I ever applied for; the moments as a child that I was sad about my parents' divorce and yet an invisible force came to comfort me. Now the force had made itself known, loud and clear. I could no longer deny it. Some people could label this a religious experience but I resisted the temptation to create a story about the feelings I had had and instead felt curious and open for more, whatever that would look like.

This new openness helped me become more sensitive. I got invited to a party with Mani and his friends, most of who were quite a bit older than myself and had known each other a long time. I recall walking down the path towards the house where the party was held and feeling an interesting thickness to the air. Inside the house people were engaged in intimate, lively conversations, some were snuggling in hammocks, others were hugging or massaging each other in an intimate way that was totally foreign to me as a Brit.

What had I walked into? Some kind of old-hippy nirvana?

That buzzing feeling in the air grew even more intense. I felt a bit 'high', yet hadn't drunk a thing. I found Mani over by the punch bowl and asked him about it.

"It's love you can feel," he said. "The atmosphere here is literally charged with it."

Once I knew the feeling of love, I could recognize it at other times under other circumstances. It had an elevating effect on me; my body felt as though it was vibrating more rapidly. It felt just plain better and I knew I wanted a LOT more of THAT!

I stayed three glorious weeks in Yelapa, made many friends and planned on coming back again after my journey through the Americas. It was in my head at that point to travel for about another year, then take the Tran-Siberian express back to Moscow and fly home to London to become a shiatsu therapist. I had done a course in shiatsu therapy in London before I'd left and had loved both receiving and giving this Japanese form of massage, performed fully clothed and with no oil. But, to paraphrase an ancient German proverb, *Mann denkt, Gott lenkt* – or... if you want to make God laugh, show her your plans!

Chapter 4

Dateline: Summer 1988
Harbin Hot Springs

I spent four more months touring Mexico, Belize and Guatemala and eventually made my way back to California in May 1988. A friend I had met on the beach at Yelapa, Bo, had invited me to visit when in Los Angeles and I spent a month hanging out in Manhattan Beach with Bo and his buddies. LA was fun, but I was anxious to continue my journey so in June I headed north to the Bay area.

While I was in San Francisco, I came across a magazine called *Common Ground*. It was a New Age kind of publication with a myriad of healers, therapists, psychics and massage people advertising their skills. I flicked through the magazine and saw an ad for a course in Shiatsu Therapy at a place called Harbin Hot Springs. No websites in those days, print ads and phone calls were it! But although I knew nothing about the place, something appealed to me about this course and I made a phone call. Before I knew it, I was registered for a course starting in August. That left two months to explore Oregon, Washington, Canada and Alaska!

I visited Cathy and Kevin in Ashland, Oregon and spent a delightful week with them practicing yoga in their studio and discovering the Shakespeare theaters and Lithia Park. I hitchhiked north to Seattle, a great jumping off point for the ferry to Victoria, Canada. From there I hitched a ride on a plane – yes, really! The guy who picked me up was heading to the airport and flying the length of Vancouver Island, saving me a day of road travel. We left his vehicle at a small airport and boarded a tiny seaplane, which he piloted for the one-hour flight north. From there, I took the ferry to

Alaska, but it rained so I only spent one day in Ketchikan and before hopping the next ferry back to Canada. I visited Banff and Jasper for wonderful hiking then started to head back south. I had an appointment in California.

And so it came to pass that one hot August evening, I found myself hitching a ride from the sleepy country town of Middletown to this mysterious Harbin Hot Springs to start my massage classes. The grizzled man at the entrance gate sported a long gray beard and was wearing a tie-dyed shirt. He checked me in and gave me a map of the property.

"If you don't have a tent, you'll be wanting to sleep out on the deck under the stars," he said. "But mind the skunks, they're quite friendly but don't like to be bothered unexpectedly."

I walked wearily up the hill with my backpack still on, passing a garden and gazebo area. Intoxicating aromas of lavender, dried grasses and herbs floated on the twilight air. I passed delightful-looking grounds surrounded by turn-of-the-century-style rooms, illuminated by small lights, giving the landscape a fairly-tale quality. Luscious green lawns shaded by giant oak trees sheltered a troop of chattering quail. A girl passed me. She had dreadlocks and smelled of musk oil. She wore an exotic flowing kind of outfit.

Hmm, what's going on here? A "Summer of Love reunion?" Where do people buy clothes like that anyway? Retro stores?

I climbed higher up the hill, to a deck area by a swimming pool... and to my surprise, saw a naked person! And another... and another!

Oh my God! It's a nudist resort! Who knew? What would my Victorian – era grandmother say about all this?

Fairy-tale land had turned into Fellini! Now I'm not one to be prudish about such matters, but a warning would have been nice!

Once I got over the shock that the people around the swimming pool were wearing nothing but smiles, there was really nothing to do but join them! After all, I was hot and dusty and needed a dip. Rather self-consciously, I stripped off and made my way to another of the pools.... ahhhh – this one was deliciously warm! It felt like liquid silk on my skin and enveloped my weary bones with its tender, watery embrace. Others were relaxing in the pool, which was large enough to hold at least forty people. I looked up at the starry sky, melted into that silken water and really felt like I had died and gone to heaven! Tiny bubbles of hydrogen peroxide gathered on my skin like champagne bubbles and I was fascinated by their feel on different parts of my body. Relaxing now, I looked around, absorbing the scene. I noticed a beautiful vase of fresh flowers at one end of the pool and to the left of it, a mysterious entrance to another hall.

Curious, I climbed the steps up out of the warm pool and into the next chamber. Inside was a smaller pool, steam rising from its waters. I dipped a toe in. *Ouch!* It was steaming hot! Yet a couple of people were resting quietly here too, so feeling encouraged, I very gingerly made my way into this hot pool to soak... and came face to face with the Goddess.

I have no idea what her name is, or how she got there. Her face is exquisitely carved in stone and she sits above the hot pool framed in a small window, illuminated by flickering candles, smiling her Mona Lisa smile at all who venture near her watery kingdom. Someone had placed a crown of flowers on her head and beneath her was a metallic dolphin, water spouting from his mouth. I was entranced. It was as though she spoke to me that starry, hot August night, saying, "Welcome home, Julia. You will receive many blessings here."

I fell in love with Harbin from that moment on. Something inside me resonated deeply with this land, this pure water, with the loving care that had been poured into every facet of Harbin life. My body buzzed with the recognition that I had discovered a place that was to me meaningful to me for the rest of my life, even though on that first night, I would have no clue as to what that would mean.

After soaking in those magical pools, I discovered the restaurant and ate my first of many fabulous organic, fresh-cooked vegetarian meals on the deck overlooking the valley below. I picked up my meal at the counter and found a space at a table outside. The air was warm and the food was delicious. Home-baked bread and butter melted in my mouth to accompany the picked-that-day salad and freshly made vegetable soup. A fellow diner asked me if I knew what movie was playing that night!

A movie theater? Here? How cool was that!

After dinner, tired and happy, I followed him down to the small building next door where the movies were screened and sank down onto the comfy, cozy cushions in the theater, watching a movie with about forty others, trying to stay awake till the end.

Later, I laid my sleeping bag out on the wooden upper deck and stared up at the stars. I must have been pretty hardy; no pad or air mattress for me! Yet I hardly noticed the hard wood beneath me. I was entranced by the night's sky, the sounds, the smells and how relaxed I already felt.

Sure enough, I soon heard the patter of tiny feet! Little black and white skunks were scampering around, sniffing peoples' packs and looking for food! I lay totally still, scared to disturb them in case they decided I was unfriendly and sprayed me. They did not. I relaxed and stopped worrying, and quickly fell asleep.

The next morning after breakfast I made my way to one of the workshop buildings to start my course. Harold Dull was the teacher, an older man with a long gray beard and laconic way of speaking. We learned the meridians, pressure points and all kinds of ways of stretching and opening the body, Japanese style. It was wonderful! Two weeks of heavenly bliss being massaged, giving massage, soaking in the tubs, making new friends and getting to know this magical Harbin.

Each morning at 7:00 a.m. we had water shiatsu class (wat-su) in the warm pool. We would stand in the warm water and take turns floating each other, adding stretches and massage moves as we cradled our partner in our arms. There was only one problem. I am 5ft 4 inches and had to stand on tiptoes to keep my chin above the water, which left me unstable. I'm ashamed to say, this resulted in me dunking the head of my guinea pig on numerous occasions! Still it was a magical experience to receive the floating and rocking, like being back in the womb - warm, safe, nurturing and totally relaxing.

I found out that Harbin was really "The Church of Heart Consciousness" and not strictly a nudist resort, just clothing optional at the pools or at the weekly dance. It was more a New Age Disneyland for adults. There were about a hundred residents who lived and worked on the property. They were a mixed bunch; most were looking for an antidote to civilization. Some were escaping bad marriages or unfulfilling careers; others were using their time here as a step in their recovery. Then there were the healers, the massage therapists, the yoga teachers, the breath-work people; and the hippies. There was no smoking except in a special pavilion, no drugs and no alcohol. I did not miss all that one bit, there was so much going on every day. Apart from our classes and the daily movies, there were hiking trails, dances in the main hall, meditation groups, yoga classes, chanting sessions and guest speakers.

It soon became clear to me that I needed to adjust to this Californian culture. My boisterous A-type personality would not go down well here. I noticed that when people greeted each other, they looked deeply into each other's eyes and gave each other long melting hugs. No one wore make-up or fussed with their hair. Girls did not wear bras, hell, I don't think they even wore deodorant! People were *au naturel* in all ways.

And I loved it! Yes, I LOVED those hippies! I may have still sounded like a middle-class Londoner but I soon adapted to their free-flowing ways. I discovered I LOVED swimming naked – it felt so sensual and freeing. I enjoyed the long hugs and the warmth I felt in my heart at such greetings. I relinquished my diet of pizza and cereal and learned about the value of eating organic, locally grown food. It took just a few days to feel more alive and vibrant from this healthy diet coupled with daily yoga, soaking and massage.

The two weeks of my shiatsu class sped by in a glorious haze of touch, laughter and hot-tubbing. I could not bring myself to leave when it ended, so I didn't. I signed up for a Swedish massage class and stayed another week. After that, I just hung out, enjoying the place, my new friends and practicing my new skills.

Sometimes I would hike to the Tea House, a small meditation hut in the hills with a great view of the valley below. It was calm and peaceful up there, nestled amongst the manzanita trees, and the mind could naturally quieten and drop into a peaceful meditative state.

Or I would go and sit by the secret waterfall that was hidden behind the hotel building. Cool water cascaded over the rocks and a large fig tree spread its roots and limbs over the hill like a giant spider offering a shady respite from the summer heat.

Thursday was "Unconditional Dance" night, alternative culture at its finest! All age groups, shapes and sizes moving and grooving to the beat of their own drums. Some people morphed their movement into yoga-like postures, others moved like wild animals, completely naked. Most dancers danced alone, absorbed in their own movement and self-expression. Some formed couples or pods of three or four, rubbing themselves playfully against each other with all parts of their bodies. It was joyful and delightful and I loved it! In London I had never been one to dress up and hit the clubs. On the rare occasion that I had gone, I noticed the girls all posturing, waiting to be asked to dance, then performing some kind of self-conscious, embarrassed shuffle, devoid of any passion or presence. But here I could literally undress and just have fun, letting my body express itself however it needed, without trying to impress or conform.

The Harbin store sold "goddess clothes." I embraced my inner hippy and bought myself some flowing purple pants and a colorful halter-top. Now I even looked the part. And as time wore on, I felt those old, conditioned parts of myself dropping away like a snakeskin until a new me emerged, a clearer, freer, more authentic me, softer, less intellectual, more open.

And one day I disappeared.

At least it seemed that way. Michael, one of the residents, was a *re-birther*. He had befriended me and offered me a session. I had never even heard of rebirthing let alone done any, so intrigued, I accepted his invitation. I lay down and he suggested I start breathing deeply, a connected breath where I breathed in more quickly than usual. Michael kept encouraging me. "Keep breathing, stay with the rhythm. Yes, that's it."

I breathed, I breathed, I breathed.... and then I started to experience my arm pulsating, then my entire body vibrating. I was aware of that and how odd it felt ... and then all of a sudden, I was gone. No one was there to be aware of anything. I simply melted. Disappeared. I have no clue where I went or how long I was gone. At some point I returned to consciousness the same way I had gone out, becoming aware of the vibrating mass of the body first, then slowly as the pulsing slowed down, feeling the physical body again, then opening my eyes and seeing Michael's smiling face staring down at me. Wow. I felt amazing - refreshed, open, alive. I had no idea breathing could be this transforming!

Harbin worked its magic on me and I stayed well into September. I had this strong feeling that I was meant to live near this sacred place. I had no clue why, but it seemed to be important, as though the Goddess herself would be continually luring me back, for some mysterious purpose of her own.

I had entered the USA on a tourist visa and it was rapidly running out. I had to get myself back across the border by early November, so I could head back down to Yelapa again and spend the winter in my favorite Mexican village before the journey home to London. With a heavy heart, I tore myself away to start the long journey south, passing back through Bo's house in Los Angeles, Shelly's house in San Diego and eventually returning to Mexico. I arrived back in Yelapa on December 6th, 1988.

46

Chapter 5

Dateline: December 1988
Yelapa

As the taxi boat from Vallarta turned the corner into
Yelapa bay, my heart leaped with joy. It felt like a
homecoming, a familiar friendly place in a year of new and
foreign. This time I knew the ropes. After landing on the
beach I walked to Valentino's restaurant and asked about a
casita to rent.

"Si Senorita," said Valentino. Very close and very
cheap... you come look."

He led me behind the row of beach eateries, past where
the donkeys wait to take American tourists up to the
waterfall, down the sandy path a few yards and opened an
old, wooden gate. It opened into a small yard area with a
palapa shack. He let me inside. After last years' experience,
I was not in as much shock as I would have been otherwise.
A swinging bed hung from rafters with a mosquito net
covering an old mattress. The bathroom was a hole in the
floor leading to God knows where. There was a kitchen of
sorts, with a couple of grubby looking coffee cups, a
beaten-up saucepan and a gas canister for heating water...
but where was the water?

"You have your own personal well!" Valentino
exclaimed proudly. He took me outside and showed me the
well... a dark, musty-smelling hole with a dirty bucket
attached to a rope that would descend noisily down into the
depths of the water table to procure precious H2O.
"You use for toilet, cooking and washing."

OK. I gulped. I could do that... for $100 a month it was
well within my budget and a stone's throw away from that

47

gorgeous beach. Anyway the view over the lagoon was charming. I gave him a deposit and promptly moved in.

Actually I loved my swinging bed. I bought some sheets and a pillowcase and at night could rock myself to sleep listening to the waves roll up on the beach. I slept wonderfully deep and sound.

The first morning, I woke up, lifted the edge of the mosquito net and screamed! The floor was littered with scorpions! At first I thought they were alive and wondered how I would cross the floor to get my shoes without getting stung. But as I looked closer, I realized they were all dead as doornails. They had fallen down from the thatched roof at night and lay strewn across the floor, tiny and white but with deadly venom if you were unlucky enough to get stung.

Gingerly, I walked around them, found a broom and swept them away. That was the last time I walked around without shoes and a flashlight at night! I should mention, too, that at that time Yelapa had no electricity. In some ways the village was quite proud of this fact. It helped keep major tourism away and maintained the charm of the village as houses were lit by candles and gas lamps at night. The Yacht Club, the hotel and a couple of nicer houses had generators to create electricity for showers and stereos, but mostly everyone just made do with lighting sources from a bygone era. It was DARK at night, so a flashlight was absolutely necessary for navigating the narrow lanes through the village and out towards the point.

Looking a little closer at the kitchen, I resolved to do no cooking at all! It just didn't look safe or hygienic. Besides, the beach restaurants were close, cheap and fabulous! I threw on shorts and T-shirt and headed off to find breakfast. Actually I had a game plan for my extended stay in Yelapa. Now I was a trained massage therapist, I thought I could ply my wares on the beach and make some extra cash treating tourists. I also thought it would be fun to offer t'ai chi classes on the beach some mornings, as I had been studying in London and loved those slow, graceful movements. After breakfast, I noticed a couple of local

48

gringo friends lying on the sand and went over to see them.

"Hi Joe, hi Sam. I'm back! Hey, do you know anyone would like me to demonstrate some massage on them right here on the beach? I have a great technique for walking on the back and if I can show people, it will be easier for me to get some clients."

"Oh man, I would LOVE you to walk on my back!"

I looked past Joe to see whom this rich, smooth voice belonged to and saw a friendly, smiling American guy about thirty with red shorts and a buffed, hairless chest, a thick mop of curly brown hair and a deep tan. He had the most beautiful bright blue eyes I'd ever seen.

"OK, lie down right here on the sand, put your hands down by your side and turn your head to the right."

I placed my foot on his sacrum and started to rock him. People stopped to watch. I was being a bit of show-off, so stepped up onto his back and started pressing up his back with my left foot, holding onto Sam for balance.

"Exhale deeply as I press down. Yes, that's it. And again."

It was like surfing, but on a back rather than on a wave. And it feels SO good to have it done!

"What's your name anyway," I asked, once I had hopped off and he could speak.

"Well the locals call me Antonio. But I'm just Tony. How about you? Is that an Australian accent?"

"I'm Julia and I'm English. Don't worry – most Americans think I'm an Aussie because I'm blonde."

"Wow that massage felt really good. Where did you learn to do that? Japan?"

"Actually London first. I took a course in barefoot shiatsu there then studied some more at Harbin Hot Springs in California last summer."

"I'm from California – my parents live in Tahoe. I come down every winter for the fishing. How long are you

49

staying?"

"Not sure really... my money will run out at some point and I'll have to head back to London but I'm hoping to at least ride out the winter down here."

"Well you're a girl to marry... just imagine having a massage like that every day!"

I felt a chill run through my body. What an odd thing to say.

A couple of people watching asked me if I was free to give them a treatment and before too long I had clients lined up. I was thrilled. It gave me something to do that I loved and some extra cash to finance my stay. I thanked Tony for being my "victim" and he offered me a drink.

"Don't mind if I do," I replied, "it's thirsty work giving massage!"

We settled into one of the beach bars and got chatting. We chatted about our past and I found out his mother was German and his father was Latvian and he spoke German fluently, as his family used to live there.

"Du sprichst Deutsch! Wie shoen! Wir koennen miteinander Deutsch reden!" (You speak German? How lovely! We can talk German together!) I had studied German at University and lived in Vienna for a year so was thrilled to be able to practice my language skills.

Tony was warm, charming and interesting. The day wore on but our conversation did not wear out. I started to feel as though there was no one else on the beach. We were creating our own little bubble of energy and it felt delicious. He seemed to know everyone in the bar and started introducing me to friends.

"Julia you must meet Pedro, he takes me fishing most mornings. And Maria, she's Carmen the pie lady's daughter. And this is Rick, he lives up on the Point near Isabel's place. And that's David... hey come join us for a drink." Tony had that rare quality of making everyone feel like they were his best friend. I could see these other guys

50

adored him, hung on his every word. He had the charisma of a born leader, the charm of a Casanova and I found myself already intrigued with him.

Tony asked how I came to be in Yelapa and I told him how I had met Kathy, Kevin and Mia the previous year and how we landed here all together.

"Mia?" he asked, "Is she African American by chance?"

"Yes" I said, wide-eyed, "How did you know that?"

"She was on a boat with me and some friends in Cabo last year for a few days. Then she left to get the ferry to the mainland. I lost track of her after that. That's when you must have met her."

Now that was a coincidence! I have learned to always be on the look out for coincidences like this one, I mean really, what were the chances? I have this idea that when my spirit guides want me to really pay attention, when something is really important for me to see, they lay a coincidence in my lap. Here was one I could not ignore.

We both took a little longer look at each other than was socially acceptable in polite society. *What could this mean?*

Morning slipped into afternoon and eventually I had to excuse myself to go and give a massage.

"See you later at the Yacht Club," yelled Tony as I left for my appointment. It was Saturday and the whole town would be there later for the twice-weekly dance.

It had been an idyllic day of new friends and new possibilities on my dream beach. I had been traveling alone for some time and now it felt so good to have landed somewhere for a bit and make connections that would ensure my social calendar remained full for weeks to come.

I noticed I took a little more care than usual with deciding what to wear that night. My choices were limited.

Oh God everything is wrinkled and looks shabby! I stared forlornly at the contents of my red backpack emptied out on the swinging bed. The old pair of hippy-style, gray

51

baggy pants would not do. The green ones were a little more sexy but filthy dirty. Ah, the red dress from Greece! I had bought this dress a few years ago in Rhodes when invited to an impromptu dinner party and being informed that David Gilmour of Pink Floyd would be coming. I had nothing to wear so ran out and bought a rather fetching Greek-style red frock. David turned up in baggy jeans and an old blue sweatshirt. We argued all night long over curry and retsina about politics and religion, getting drunk as skunks and having a generally rip-roaring time. Anyway it had resulted in my procurement of the red dress. It was a bit wrinkled but would do. I found some sandals, grabbed cash and a flashlight and headed up the beach towards the village. It's about a twenty-minute walk and by the time I arrived at the Yacht Club, the place was humming with activity and in full on dinner-service mode.

"Hey Jules. We're over here!" I looked over and saw Tony sitting with Joe and Sam at a table overlooking the picturesque little bay.

He called me Jules, my London nickname. It felt familiar and inviting.

"Hi! May I join you for dinner?" I always tend to go for polite formality even though I felt fairly certain it would be okay.

Tony was already up and getting me a chair. "Sit down and join us. The fish tonight is mahi-mahi and it was just caught this morning."

Three lovely gentlemen to chat with, fresh fish, an amazing location... I was in heaven.

I was definitely the curiosity of the evening. The others were all American and I have noticed a certain intrigue that they have for the mystery and (relative?) sophistication of European women. I, on the other hand, was bowled over by the openness of American men, their friendly manners, generosity and playfulness. They spelled FUN and were quite different from the more formal men I had met in London over recent years.

52

We ate the most delicious dinner and afterwards the music cranked up and it was time for dancing! The local Mexicans were all standing around checking out the scene but as soon as the DJ started to play Mexican beat music, they leaped onto the dance floor and impressed us Westerners with their nifty dance moves! (I use the term Westerner to describe North Americans and Europeans). One of them grabbed me and tried to teach me Mexican two-step. What fun! It wasn't so hard to pick up and soon I was swirling around the dance floor with the locals!

After a while the music changed to rock and roll. The Mexicans slunk back into the shadows and now the Westerners were up. The Rolling Stones were cranking out "Satisfaction" and Tony took my hand and led me back to dance. He LOVED to dance! And I loved that he loved to dance. We had such fun gyrating and boogying together, until the early hours; I felt my whole being expand into a wonderful feeling of pure joy. This was as good as it gets. A slow dance came on. He pulled me in towards him and I lay my head on his shoulder, nestling into his muscular chest.

Mamma – this feels good.

The dance wound down about midnight and exhausted, I headed back up the hill to the beach and my scorpion-infested palapa.

The next day, I could hardly wait to get down to the beach and see Tony.

He wasn't there. I had no idea how to find him either! I didn't know where he lived, no one had a phone; hell, I didn't even know his last name! I went about my day, gave a couple of massages and was just thinking about where I was going to have dinner when I saw Tony walking down the beach. I felt a wave of relief at seeing him. He walked towards me and asked if I would have a drink with him.

"Sure," I said trying to remain cool and collected. "Mine's a pina colada. Where have you been all day anyway?" I could not hide my curiosity.

"Well I went fishing this morning, then took a nap in my hammock. Went shopping to get some food for tonight as I have a very special guest coming for dinner."

"Who?" I asked, slightly alarmed.

"You!"

That was smooth. I tried to remain calm but my insides were doing cartwheels.

"Hmmm, let me check my calendar." I feigned digging in my beach bag for a book and consulting it with all seriousness, said, "You are in luck. I appear to be free tonight. So how do I find your *palapa?*"

"You go through the village past the Yacht Club towards the Point, turn left onto the small trail that goes up the hill by the market, right at the black pig, left again at the big, white pig, then mine is the second house up the hill from there. You will see the terrace and smell the garlic shrimp cooking."

White pig, black pig. Jeepers... would I be able to find this place? What kind of directions were they?

And yet, they were right on! There really was a big black pig in a stall that was immediately obvious as I walked up the hill; and an even bigger white pig, well, it was grubby and cream-colored but I got the idea; I really could smell the garlic shrimp cooking as I made my way huffing and puffing up the steep trail to Tony's house.

My God! What a view! It was stunning to see the sweep of the bay from Tony's terrace. It was dusk and gaslights were starting to flicker in the distance illuminating the little village.

"Oh you're here! Fantastic!" Tony made me feel like the most welcome guest in the world. "Perfect timing. The rice is about done and the shrimp are cooked."

I stepped into a neat little house and saw a relatively (for Yelapa) well-stocked kitchen with pots on the stove and a bottle of wine and glasses at the ready. I was impressed.

"Can I help you with anything?"

"No just go sit outside. I'll have it all served up in a few."

I waited on the terrace basking in my good luck. I had effortlessly and easily met a charming man who was cooking me dinner in this most beautiful of places. Life was GOOD!

The food was great. We ate, talked, drank and relaxed into each other's company. But at the end of dinner when we were clearing up, I noticed something strange. Tony did not seem able to see where everything was. He put his hand out to grab a dish and did not connect with it right away.

"Can you see OK? Do you need more light?" I asked innocently.

"Well, Jules, that's a story. Actually, no, I do not see that well. I have something called *macular degeneration*. It means I can see through the corner of my eyes but not directly ahead. I'm officially legally blind but I can function just fine really."

Wow. That was different. Yet I didn't feel one bit bothered about Tony's disability, just made a mental note to warn him of stray scorpions or rocks on the trail he may not see. And those eyes, so blue and clear... I looked at him long and deep and saw no sign of anything wrong. In fact, I saw something else; a beautiful man with a twinkle in his eye looking back at me with love. He took my hand and drew me closer right there on the terrace. Our lips met and he kissed me, long and slow. We must have kissed for about five minutes before I came up for air.

What was that? I felt a shiver run through my spine.

He led me over to the hammock and we lay down together, cuddled up against the cooling breeze. Have you ever tried to get two people comfortable in a hammock? Not the easiest task in the world! We rolled and giggled and maneuvered and laughed... eventually ending up with limbs twisted around each other like human pretzels, melting into each other, no longer knowing where one arm ended and one leg began. As we kissed and cuddled and laughed and talked, it was as though we had entered sacred time, a blissful space where nothing else in the world mattered except the feel of our bodies wrapped together, the scent of the fragrant night air and the sound of the waves below.

I have no idea how long we laid together in that hammock, but at some point I felt it was time to head back to my beach shack on my own. After all, this was our first date. Reluctantly, I grabbed my cardigan and flashlight and kissed him goodnight, steeling myself for the long walk home.

****

I woke up the next morning with warm, fuzzy feelings in my heart. Memories of the night before came flooding back and I lingered in my swinging bed, reluctant to disturb my delicious reverie. Tony said he would see me on the beach at lunchtime so I went about my business that morning, trying to calm down those butterflies of excitement in my belly.

Things moved swiftly with us after that. It was as if we both knew we were meant to be together and it was just a given; no need to date further or have any doubt about "if" or "whether." Our relationship was consummated three days later on my swinging bed with little fanfare and almost a sense of normalcy about it. Bells did not ring in my head, we were not even hugely compatible in the sexual arena, but that did not matter. Sexual attraction was clearly not the main factor drawing us together, it was something much deeper; a sense of recognition, comfortable familiarity, an agreement. Above all, we both had this overwhelming knowing that we were destined for each other.

Nine days after we met, Tony proposed to me. No engagement ring... just a cheap, Mexican bracelet he had found at the local market.

"This will have to do until we get back to the States and I can find you something nicer."

I didn't care. Material objects and fine jewelry have never meant that much to me. I rarely wear much in the way of adornment, neither make-up nor jewelry, and don't even have pierced ears.

To my own amazement, I heard myself saying, "YES! Of course I will marry you!"

There was absolutely NO doubt in my mind. None whatsoever.

As a sensible, logical, intelligent young lady, I could have had second thoughts. Here I was betrothing myself to a blind guy who lived off social security at that time and who owned nothing in the world except a gauze Mexican shopping bag with a pair of red shorts and two T-shirts. That was it. Oh and some flip-flops. Tony was as minimal as you could get! But that had no bearing on my decision. In fact, it just seemed like the most natural thing in the world to be marrying this man I hardly knew, to be writing to my parents that I would be leaving the UK for good and moving to California and getting married to someone they had never heard of! My poor parents must have been SO shocked!

Yet he had qualities that are hard to find and that I was strongly attracted to. For a start, Tony was a happy soul. He always had a smile on his face and lifted the spirits of all around him. He was a strong, alpha male, and as a strong female, I need a powerful man who I can trust, lean into and relax with. It brought out my feminine side and I loved that. We were nearly the same age. I was just a year older.

Tony told me that he had never expected to live much past thirty, as he had taken so many dangerous risks in his life. He really was a person who had NO fear and had done lots of crazy exploits, especially given his limited vision. He had lost half a toe in a biking accident but was otherwise fairly unscathed. For him, living past thirty felt like bonus time so he saw every day as a blessing and lived it to the full, with open heart, joy and non-attachment. Now that was rare!

He had something else to tell me that day as well.

"Jules, I am so sorry to leave you but I have to go back to the States for Christmas. I will come back as soon as I can, but my family is expecting me and I already have my ticket."

I was taken aback, but trusted that he would hurry back to Yelapa and we would spend the winter together in Mexico.

"When are you leaving?"

"The day after tomorrow. I can't wait to tell my family all about you – they are going to LOVE you!"

Tony left, promising to return soon but unable to give me a firm return date. I was left in my beach shack, and the life I had created for myself on the beach. I taught t'ai chi on Tuesday and Friday mornings to two students, Sarah and Maureen, who enjoyed this as a lovely way to start the day. I was still offering massages to locals that helped to keep me in margaritas and was continuing to expand my group of friends, getting invited almost daily to a lunch, tea party or gathering of some kind around the bay.

One day, I was about to go up to Lang's house to give a couple of treatments to some of his houseguests when I suddenly felt ill, sick to my stomach.

Drat – those prawns I had last night must have been old.

I went to my hole in the ground and promptly threw up. Thinking a good vomit was all I needed to clear my system, I headed up to Lang's house and started my shiatsu. Half way through the second treatment, I felt sick again. Breathing deep, I just managed to complete the treatment before dashing to the loo and puking again. Ugh! I felt awful!

The next day was Christmas and lots of parties were happening around the various restaurants and homes of Yelapa. I started to feel better and assumed I'd just had food poisoning, so ate and drank as normal. But then a few days afterwards, I woke up feeling like I had the flu, but a really bad flu. I felt achy and tired and had no appetite.

Where was Tony when I needed him? I really could have used some support right about now. He had been gone nine days already and I was beginning to wonder if this whole marriage idea was just a dream. Would he even come back? Was he just a bullshit artist who led women on? I honestly didn't know.

I dragged myself over to the beach restaurant to get a bottle of water and saw Valentino.

"*Hola* Julia. Antonio is here... see?" He pointed down the beach and sure enough, Tony had just arrived by boat and was walking down to find me.

Oh God – and I feel like crap!

Still I was overjoyed to see him. My heart danced a jig and I summoned up some hidden energy reserve to run up and give him a big hug and a kiss.

"I've missed you SO much! And I have SO much to tell you! My parents can't wait to meet you and I have presents for you!" he said excitedly.

The words tumbled out and were sweet music to my ears. We walked back to my shack.

" I think I've got the flu, I hate to pass it on to you."

"In sickness and in health, sweetheart. I will eat your measly flu. Bring it on!"

So we reunited and my joy in seeing him helped me recover my energy somewhat.

But the next day when I woke up, something was clearly wrong. I felt even worse and started to pee black. Now that is a weird thing, peeing black. It's supposed to be clear or a little bit yellow, but black? What the hell was wrong with me? I was running a temperature and ached badly. Then when I pooped it came out white. Now I knew I was in trouble.

There was an American doctor called Gerard who lived

way up river, about forty minutes walk from my hut. Luckily he was hanging out on the beach that day and Tony went to find him to get him to look at me.

"She's got hepatitis. She needs rest, lots of liquids and warm showers. She really shouldn't stay here. Keep an eye on her and let me know how she is."

Oh God. This was not good. There was no way I was capable of going back to Puerto Vallarta on a boat. We needed a miracle.

So Tony did his magic. He walked around the beach area to establish where there were hot showers -only two places – Lang's house and the large white house on the hill, the *Casa Blanca*. He tracked down the owner of the *Casa Blanca* and found out he was going back to the States for a month and needed someone to house sit. He volunteered us!

"Settled!" he announced proudly, on returning to my *casita*. "We're moving in today. We will get you in a nice clean bed and you will have a warm shower by this afternoon."

But I still had to get there. You may recall, there are no cars in Yelapa. You pretty much have to walk everywhere. We took a boat across the little bay to the village to save me walking too far, but then I had to stagger up the path that led to the Point to where the steps lead up to the *Casa Blanca*. There are one hundred and forty steps up to the house. It was about 2.00pm and a warm day. I will never forget how painful that walk was. Each step was agony, as by then I had such a high temperature that I could hardly move. Tony helped me, pushing me up as best he could. Finally we arrived at the house. I fell into a bed and stayed there for a week, getting weaker and weaker.

It was odd, sitting up there on the hill feeling the life force drain out of me. I felt completely detached from everything. Time dragged by in a haze and I restlessly fell in and out of sleep. After seven days, I was not looking good. Although the doctor had said that there is nothing you can do to treat hepatitis and it just heals eventually,

Tony was worried.

"Right. That's enough. I am going to get some transport and go find Gerard."

In true cavalier fashion, he procured a mule, rode up river and returned a couple of hours later with Gerard in tow. The good doctor examined my weak, ailing body with concern.

"She's severely dehydrated. You need to go into PV as quickly as possible and get her a drip and fluids."

It was too late to get there and back in one day. Somehow I made it through another miserable night and the next thing I remember is Tony and Gerard and an elderly Mexican lady sitting by my bed setting the drip up.

As the fluids dripped into me, I could feel the life force returning. Four hours I lay there, until the bags were empty and my body was re-hydrated. What a difference! I perked up almost immediately. And not a moment too soon. It was hot, I was sweating and it had been hard to drink enough. I had faced a very real possibility of dying from dehydration.

I slowly got well. I had lost twenty pounds and had got quite thin, but about ten days later, felt well enough to walk into town and do some gentle yoga at the twice weekly class at Miki Shapiro's place. I slowly regained my infamous appetite. Now I was starving, literally! I ate everything in sight!

Tony was thrilled I was getting better.

"Jules, lets plan an engagement party! We can have it up here at the *Casa Blanca* and it can be our send-off before we head back to the States."

Now if there's one thing I love, it's planning parties! I swear just the idea of that helped my energy! Word soon spread of our engagement and a date was set for late January. One of our friends made a cake of two rings joined together all in chocolate. We asked everyone to bring food for a potluck and musical instruments.

Over sixty people showed up. We had the most magical

evening in that house with the great view on the hill. Toasts were drunk, promises to return soon were made and it turned out to be a heart-warming Yelapa-style send-off for us both. People really wished us well in our new life.

We sat up on the terrace after everyone had gone and Tony said, " Well, sweetheart, what shall we do when we get back to California?"

"I want to do massage. I can't wait to get my own practice going."

"And I want to do Real Estate. After all, if you're going to sell something, you might as well sell the biggest thing you can and make more money!"

We left Yelapa on February 6th 1989 and made our way north from the tropics to the snows of Lake Tahoe.

****

Tony did have a wonderful family and we all got along extremely well. We spent the next few weeks getting to know each other and planning the wedding. My parents were somewhat surprised at this turn of events but nevertheless, my Dad was brave enough to fly out and marry off his eldest daughter!

On March 19th, 1989, in The Church of the Snows, Squaw Valley, Tahoe, wearing a simple white dress and a tiara of flowers, I linked arms with my dear Dad and walked down the aisle. It was a perfect spring day and the sun shone through the stained glass window of the little church and made a halo around Tony, waiting at the altar, looking dapper in his tux and flanked by his brother, Peter, and best friend, Thomas, who later married my sister, Lisa. My heart was bursting with joy, yet at the same time, I remember so clearly the thought, "it won't last." That didn't matter. I knew I had to do this; and I was happy about my decision, gaily optimistic despite that foreboding thought.

After a dream honeymoon in Kauai, we moved to

Sacramento (where I live to this day). This was the first time I had created a home of my own and I loved it. Tony and I were very compatible together as we are both social people and we soon had lots of friends. We both got our Real Estate licenses and built up a real estate business. I developed a massage practice... and ended up living two hours away from Harbin Hot Springs, near enough to go and visit the Goddess whenever I felt like it.

****

And that Bob, is how this bar changed my life, how I met my husband and got to live in America,"

"Then what happened?" asked Bob.

"We were blissfully happy for about three years and then as the housing market dived in the early nineties, life became more stressful and some aspects of our marriage that were not working became clearer. The last two years were not so great and things started to fall apart.

"And where is Tony now?"

" He is happily remarried and living in Reno. Last I heard he had a successful dog grooming business."

"And how did you transition from Real Estate to yoga? Seems a bit of a leap."

"Ah well for that story we will have to travel to the Caribbean. Let's order another flan and I'll tell you what happened."

Chapter 6

Dateline February 4th, 1993
Nassau, Bahamas.

As the small ferryboat from Nassau pulled up to the jetty on Paradise Island, I felt a surge of butterflies in my stomach. Had I done the right thing, leaving home and coming here to the ashram to study yoga?

I knew I had to do something. I was completely stressed out, working five jobs to try and sustain our rapidly crumbling real estate empire and arguing with an ever more distant husband.

I had learned many valuable lessons from my marriage. "Follow what your gut knows is right", for one thing. When I had gone against that inner knowing, things had turned out badly. My instinct had been to buy two or three properties and manage them well, but Tony wanted to keep leveraging and buy more. By 1993, we were owners and part-owners of seven properties, including three large apartment buildings. Then the real estate downturn hit. Our property values dropped, renters were in arrears and soon it became clear that it was just going to be a matter of time before we, too, went into default on some of our properties.

"Never follow someone else's dreams" was the other big lesson. When I had given my power away to my husband and done what he wanted to do at the expense of my own desires, not only had I been miserable but we had ultimately failed to sustain our successes. Owning lots of real estate was not what gave me joy. It gave Tony joy, but not me. So the universe conspired to take it away, and even though at the time we both tried to hold on to it all against the odds. My passions lay in the realm of bodywork, yoga

64

and spiritual development. In June 1992, I had hosted my first stress reduction retreat weekend in the mountains of Lake Tahoe and it had been a resounding success. Three more had followed and my heart's desire was to continue creating holistic adventures.

I also made a decision never again to spend a moment of my precious time working at a job I did not enjoy. I had worked my tail off in the Real Estate world, loathed the work and in the end we had lost all the money we had made. From now on, if I was going to lose money, it would need to be earned from a task that gave me joy, not trauma.

So I thought I might become a yoga teacher. I had already taught a little yoga on the retreat weekends and had really enjoyed it. I knew it felt good in my body and was anxious to learn more. Then one day on a cold, miserable January morning, I had seen an ad for Yoga Teacher Training at the Sivananda Ashram in the Bahamas on the back of an old copy of Yoga Journal. There was a picture of a student performing a beautiful posture on a sandy beach. That was it. I was sold. I booked my flight the next day, secured my place in the February training and told my husband I was leaving.

It was hard. He told me he would not be there when I returned, that he needed to leave, spend time on his land in Oregon to figure out what was next for him and that this was the end of our marriage. Nonetheless I felt compelled to go and follow MY dream, have MY adventure, even though it meant letting go of my life with Tony and starting again. And I did LOVE living in California. I had my green card now and could stay if I wanted. I had no idea where I would go after this, but for now here I was, on a little ferry boat, sailing towards my next adventure.

A warm afternoon breeze tousled my hair as we crossed the channel separating Paradise Island from the mainland of the Nassau area. There was a bridge and you could drive over to the island too, but the ferry dropped us off very conveniently right at the ashram dock. The first thing I saw was a big sign that said "Swami Sivananada Ashram – Serve, Love, Meditate, Realize". There was a picture of

Swami Sivananda hinself, an Indian guru who had died in 1963 yet continued to inspire and teach the basics of yoga through his followers and the ashrams around the world that they had created. I liked the look of him. He had a bald head and had a big grin on his round face. If he had been alive I would have wanted to go and give him a big hug.

Next to the sign stood a dark-haired, rather portly man in orange robes. This was Swami Svaroopananda, our teacher and main man at the ashram. The Swami greeted us as we docked.

"Welcome to Sivanada Ashram. Bob and Rose will show you around and I will see you in the temple this evening." He spoke with a strong Israeli accent.

We grabbed our backpacks and Rose asked the ladies to follow her. We passed a beautiful wooden temple where our chanting and meditation meetings would be held. Opposite was a little store where we could buy goodies to supplement our diets, ice cream and chocolate being the most popular items. Further down the narrow strip of land that was the ashram, sitting as it did between the lagoon and the ocean, there were some flat, grassy lawns that served as the camping area for our tents. Tent city. Eighty people from all over the world gathered together in close quarters for a whole month to pray, pratice and learn this ancient science of yoga.

Towards the beach end of the property was the tennis court where no tennis was played and no nets were erected. It was for hatha yoga practice; the only space big enough to fit all eighty of us! Next to it was the main building which housed offices, kitchens and dining areas and beyond that, the beach deck, a smaller but very lovely wooden yoga deck overlooking the fabulous sandy beach. And that ocean - turquoise blue, warm and inviting! I couldn't wait to strip off and jump in!

But that would have to wait. First we had to collect our ashram-issue uniform of white pants and yellow T-shirts and sign up for karma yoga duty.

Karma yoga is selfless service to others. According to

the yogic texts, it is one of the four main practices of traditional yoga and serves as the foundation for the other branches of yoga, as it has the power to open the heart and purify the ego. In order to achieve this lofty goal, I was assigned to work in the ashram store for our one hour of duty a day.

"We chose you because you are a polyglot," explained Rose. "You will be able to speak to all the students in their own language." It was true. Knowing I wanted to travel from a young age, I had focussed my high school studies on languages and spoke very good German and French and passable Spanish and Italian.

"OK" I thought. "This sounds fine. I can serve ice-cream." Besides, other students were being drafted into much less appealing activities. Some had to clean the toilets, others were on dinner prep duty and some had to weed the gardens. At nineteen years old, I had spent three months on a kibbutz in Israel and had done those kinds of jobs there. It had been hard, uncomfortable work and I was glad not to have go through that again. Good. Things were going well.

Then Rose handed me the daily schedule.

Daily Schedule

6:00 a.m. Chanting and Meditation

8:00 a.m. Hatha Yoga

10:00 a.m. Brunch

12 noon Chanting class or Bhavagad Gita study

1:00 p.m. Karma Yoga

2:00 p.m. Main lecture with Swami on yoga philosophy

3:00 p.m. FREE TIME

4:00 p.m. Hatha yoga

6:00 p.m. Dinner

8:00 p.m. Chanting and Meditation...till 10:00 p.m.

What?

Chanting and meditation at 6am every day? Even on our day off? That would mean I would have to get up....even earlier than that, the crack of the very dawn, nay, still night time even!

Now I have always been a bit of a night owl. All my friends know it's fine to call me at midnight but NEVER disturb Julia before 9:00 a.m! How was I supposed to roust myself before the chickens every day? I started to think of strategies for escaping this cruel torment.... maybe I could fake sickness, forget to set my alarm.... then Rose cheerily added, "Chanting and meditation are absolutely compulsory. If you miss even once you will not be allowed to graduate."

Drat! Well, maybe it wouldn't be too bad. I would soon find out. Our first session was right after dinner. And besides, I was starving!

Dinner-time proved interesting. Before dinner we all held hands and gatherered to chant a blessing of appreciation in Sanskrit. Then we loaded our plates with salad, grains and vegies and found a place to sit and eat on the grounds or on the deck overlooking the ocean. No meat, sugar or alcohol; no onions or garlic (they were deemed too provocative a substance for aspiring yogis, as they were purported to increase the libido). Actually the food tasted great and we could eat as much as we wanted in the time alloted. I tucked into a second plate and was feeling very satisfied when the bell rang for chanting time.

I trotted off to the temple and found a seat way in the back next to a cute Canadian guy called Troy. It was to remain my spot for most of the next month. Swami came in, surrounded by eight or nine serious-looking devotees. We all sat quietly for meditation, or in my case, fidgeted, for about twenty minutes until the harmonium player sprung into action and woke everyone from whatever reverie they may have been in with a rousing rendition of "Om Namah Shivaya"!

The idea of the chanting was what is known as 'call and

response' where someone starts a chant and sings a line and everyone else joins in repeating that same line. And so on. It is suppposed to open the heart and is another of the major branches of yoga called "bhakti yoga", the yoga of devotion. I was not familiar with it and although I enjoy singing, found the melodies dreary, dull and unintelligible, being all sung in Sanskrit.

The two hours dragged interminably.

And I have to get up every day at some ungodly hour to do this? The thought did not appeal.

At 9:00 p.m. I crawled off to my tent and lay down, tired from all the traveling. I dutifully set my alarm for 5.50am (!) and tried to sleep. Then about half an hour later, I heard music. Loud music! Pop music! It sounded like it was coming from next door!

In fact it was. Club Med was right next door and started their disco at 9:30 p.m. It would have disturbed me except I was far too tired to let a little music keep me awake. I soon fell asleep.

****

It was dark and a little chilly when I was rudely awakened. *Brring! Buzzz! Beep!*

Amidst the sea of tents all parked intimately close together, the alarms started going off. In the quiet of the night I heard every one of them. I checked my watch – it was 5:25 a.m.

What is wrong with these people? Why do they need thirty minutes to get ready for temple? I was planning on a quick pee, a drink of water and the one minute stroll to my spot at the back of the room. Five minutes max with five to spare.

I tried to go back for forty more winks, but there was conversation and footsteps all around me so that was a losing battle.

OK. I'll get up!

I had forgotten about the ubiquitous line for the ladies loo. Sleepy-faced, dishevelled young girls were quietly waiting their turn for one of the two toilets in the ladies washroom. We all waited somewhat impatiently for our opportunity to relieve ourselves before shuffling down the path to temple. Somewhere nearby a cock crowed. He was sorely mistaken. Dawn was still a long way off.

I found my place at the back of the temple and Troy parked himself next to me. I gave him a nod and a wink and was glad I had made a friend already. Swami came in and meditation began. I almost nodded off again but the chairs were just uncomfortable enough to prevent that.

Then after the twenty minutes of quiet, a rasping, off-key voice started to belt out a chant. I looked at Troy and he looked at me and it was all we could do to stifle our laughter! In dirge-like fashion the remainder of the temple tried to join in, but that voice had rendered a tune impossible to follow. We were all over the place! I could hardly contain myself. This was worth getting up for! It was the funniest thing I had heard in a long time! You know how it is when you have a partner in crime? Troy and I just had to catch each others' eyes and we would be in hysterics again!

We were very, very bad. And irreverent. And I didn't care. In fact, I eventually came to enjoy our chanting time at the back of the temple, having a concealed but healthy laugh.

By and by the dawn broke. Cockerels quietened down and started looking for food. Chanting time was over. Time for hatha yoga on the tennis court.

Now we were talking! Two hours of instruction in the basics of breathing techniques and hatha yoga postures. We had a female instructor from Canada who had stood on her head every day until one day before she gave birth. I was impressed. I wanted to do that. Stand on my head I mean, not give birth.

We learned the basic deep, diaphramatic breath, alternate nostril breathing that balances the two sides of the brain, and the kapalabhati (shining skull) breath that massages the intestines and raises energy up to the crown of the head. We were taught sun salutations and the basic twelve hatha yoga postures. At the end, our teacher took us through a delicious relaxation of all the muscles in the body. I drifted off into other realms, floating in eternity, drifting through time and space... until she gently called us back into our bodies and got us sitting up ready for a final chant before completion.

I felt fantastic afterwards, open, light and relaxed. This was what I had come for! And we got to do it twice a day – oh joy! I could feel my muscles stretched out and warm and my energy expanded and flowing. I also had a humungous appetite – after all we had been up over four hours already with no food.

After breakfast we had a one hour lecture on the holy text of the yogis, the Bhavagad Gita. We mostly learned about detachment and the importance of doing your duty, imparted to us by a very serious Indian gentleman with a lilting accent that gave me some trouble following. Lord knows how the non native-English speakers amongst the student body understood a word.

Then after our hour of karma yoga duty, when I got to practice my language skills and dispense various flavors of ice-cream, film and tampons, Swami gave his lecture on yoga theory. He talked about the four paths of yoga, which are jnana yoga (wisdom yoga or self-inquiry), raja yoga and its eight limbs, one of which is hatha yoga, bhakti yoga, the devotional path of chanting and repeating the names of God, and finally karma yoga, the path of selfless service. He went on to talk about our three bodies which are the physical body, the astral body and the causal body. I was fascinated. Who knew we had all these other bodies? I certainly did not, but I came to understand that these ancient yogis knew a few things and this was a wisdom that had been handed down for the last five millenia. It all made sense and I felt innately that this philosophy was correct.

After that came our precious hour of free time, time for me to dash to the tent, change into my red bikini and run into that beautiful blue ocean. Ahhh! The best part of the day! Relaxing with a novel under a palm tree after that first delicious swim, it was hard to recollect the dramas of the life I had left behind. Already I was feeling the accumulated tensions drop from my face and body like water droplets shaken off a dog's back.

At 4:00 p.m. we were back on the tennis court for two more hours of glorious hatha yoga practice. Afternoon practice time was about learning to teach the poses. Each pose was broken down into great detail and we learned about common mistakes students would make and how to correct them. Then we had a chance to teach a couple of poses to our fellow students and get feedback on how well we were doing with our communication skills.

Such was the rhythm of our program; each day's classes building on the previous, deepening our understanding and awareness of this ancient science. Days were full, busy and stimulating and time passed quickly, moving as we did from one class to the next with barely a break in-between.

One day in the afternoon class, Jeanne was showing us the headstand. Now I have to confess, this was a pose I could not do for the life of me and in the morning class, I continued to fall over backwards, sometimes hurting myself. I was the only one of eighty students who had this issue and was feeling like a bit of a failure, so when she asked for a volunteer student to whom she could teach the pose, I raised my hand.

I brought my mat to the center of the tennis court and everyone gathered round to watch. She had me measure the distance between my elbows on the mat, interlace my fingers and place my head snugly in my palms and lift my butt to the sky. Then she invited me to start walking my feet towards my head until I could feel an uplifting sensation.

I felt an uplifting sensation alright. But it wasn't my legs, it was my T-shirt lifting up away from my navel and dropping towards my head! I had not put a bra on that morning in the dark... my bare breasts were exposed for all to see! Mortified and red-faced, I quickly came down from the pose to the muffled sniggers of all who watched. I slunk off to nurse my wounded ego outside the group while Jeanne hurriedly asked for another volunteer.

I was clearly not impressing the teaching staff.

As the days went on, I started staying up later and later to enjoy a little bit more of the fabulous tropical starry nights and it got harder and harder to get up in the mornings. On one particularly cool morning I brought my sleeping bag in to temple to wrap around me and stay warm. During the meditation, it just seemed like the obvious thing to simply slide off the chair in the back on to the floor and return to horizontal. "Sleeping-bagasana". Very cozy. And certainly conducive to a little more shut-eye at 6:00 a.m. When meditation was over, I would slink back to my chair and no-one seemed to see me. But the next day, three of the German girls also brought their sleeping bags into the temple and slithered onto the floor at meditation time. I had started a trend!

It took about five more days for Swami to catch us. From where he was perched at the front of the temple and in the dark, he could not see exactly who was sliding to the floor in the early mornings, but one day he made a general announcement that only shawls were allowed into the temple, no sleeping bags. Sleeping-bagasana was nixed.

Later that week, I was chatting to Gita, one of the other American girls, and sat next to her closer to Swami during evening chant, right above where the devotees and the musicians would sit. I liked Gita, She was a petite, pretty girl in her late twenties and a dancer with an extremely open body. Jeanne used her to demonstrate some of the more advanced hatha yoga poses and I would watch with amazement as she pretzled her way into seemingly impossible positions. She was really into the bhakti yoga so I thought I had better shape up and sing with her and everyone else. By now I was becoming more familiar with the chants and the tunes and we had been taught their

73

meanings during classes. So I gave it a go and sang my little heart out.

Then a curious thing happened.

I started to feel a glow arising in my chest that seemed to spread all over me. I felt happy, then joyful, then full-blown ecstatic! I didn't want the chant to end! Tears filled my eyes and I started to cry, not from sadness but from some upwelling of sensation I can best describe as love, which filled my being.

Oh – this is why people chant! This is what you are supposed to feel! Now I get it!

I sang loudly and joyously and the emotions kept flowing, my heart kept opening. It was delicious. I felt as though I was in love with the world, with myself, and everyone around me. It surprised the hell out of me. I gained a newfound respect for the discipline of bhakti yoga and came with more enthusiasm to temple after that experience.

On day thirteen, it was time for the six kriyas, the cleansing practices. Good yogis are encouraged to keep their insides clean as well as their outsides, hence a healthy vegetarian diet and no vices like alcohol or cigarettes. But from time to time, more extreme measures are called for, and this is where the kriyas come into play.

We were all summoned to the beach deck to watch and imitate. The first kriya was not so bad. We got a little plastic pot (neti pot) and filled it with warm salty water. Then we tilted our heads to the side and poured the water in one nostril so it came out the other one, cleasning our sinuses and nasal passages of muscous and other toxins. It felt a bit funny at first, but I quite liked this sensation of cleaning the passages. Jeanne suggested we do this daily, but twice if we think we are getting a cold or if we have a cold, as it aids in healing.

Next came the tubing up the nose. For this, we took a thin piece of red tubing and stuck it up a nostril and pulled it out through our throat, gathering excess mucous as we

74

pulled (these yogis are big on mucous). This felt even wierder but I managed to do it, at least briefly.

Then we watched as one of the teaching assistants ate a long piece of gauze, keeping one end in his mouth, then pulled the whole thing out again, effectively cleaning mucous from his oesophagus and throat. There was no way. I tried to swallow the gauze but started to gag and nearly threw up. This kriya was not going to be a regular practice for me!

Finally we were told to bring six pints of warm, salty water down to the beach front. We were to drink it all quite quickly to fill our stomachs up, then throw it all up, cleaning out the contents of our stomach. Very sexy.

So eighty of us dutifully started to pound down the warm water on the beach. Some started the puking process. Then I heard a shout in French. *"Mon Dieu! Qu'est-ce que c'est que ca?"* (Good Lord, what is that?) I turned round and saw the Club Med aerobics teacher taking his vacationers on their daily jog down the beach and they were heading our way! Bemused and shocked looking middle-class French people meet international group of puking yogis! I didn't know whether to laugh or cry, but at that instant I had absolutely no choice and felt my stomach churn as that salt water wanted to come right back out! I turned to face an oncoming wave and threw it all up!

"C'est degoulasse," (it's disgusting), I heard as I wiped my mouth. I have to say, I kind of agreed with the stuffy-looking French lady who was passing by. It was. My stomach had better stay relatively clean because I was NEVER going to do that again!

Luckily this was the only morning we were subjected to such shennanigans. However I did learn one very useful cleansing technique that I continue to do till this day. We were asked to buy our very own tongue scraper from the store and every morning scrape our tongues and remove the bacteria that accumulates there overnight. Now that I liked. It took away morning breath and left me feeling clean and pure. After a few days of developing this habit, it became unthinkable to get up and not make this the first thing I did in the bathroom. I was soon addicted to my tongue scraper! I recommend it highly!

****

The second Saturday of our training there was to be a cabaret night at the temple instead of chanting. They asked for a volunteer to be the Master of Ceremonies and being a veteran party organizer from my University days, I raised my hand and agreed to be the one to gather the performers names and introduce them all on the night.

There really was a lot of talent amongst the group. People were excited and began to practice and prepare for the big night. In fact, a few of the musicans started to gather on the beach deck after 10:00 p.m. and play and sing. Rafael, a short, young man with spectacles who hailed from Brazil, was a great guitarist. He liked to play Beatles songs and other international tunes we all knew and many of us would join in, united by the language of music. We all particularly loved his rendition of George Harrison's "My Sweet Lord" and would ask Rafael to play it over and over again. I thought it sounded like a modern day chant, the way the chorus would repeat over and over, so asked Rafael to play it at the end of our show on Saturday night.

The big day came and we were all excited. For one thing it made a change from our usual chanting, but also there were some great performers amongst us and the show was going to be really entertaining. I shook out my crumpled blue cotton dress for the occasion and at 8:00 p.m., assumed my place at the front of the temple, list of acts in hand. I grabbed the microphone and started the show, welcoming everyone in my most enthuiastic manner to the evening's entertainment.

The comedy skits were funny – some brave Argentinians imitated the Swami and his serious way of talking, mocking our yoga philosophy classes. Swami laughed along with all of us and took it in his stride. We had a couple of solo singers, some story tellers, some

76

fabulous dancers and a variety of musical pieces. I had the honor of introducing them all and getting the audience to support them with loud cheers and whistles.

Then came the final act, Rafael and his friend Andy on guitars. They started singing "My Sweet Lord". I joined in, goading the rest of the temple to do the same. Then something magical happened. Our voices rose to a crescendo, higher and louder as more and more people joined in, singing with full hearts and souls. Sensing the moment, I asked everyone to stand up and come closer together, nearer our makeshift stage. We kept singing...

I really want to see you Lord

But it takes so long my Lord

Hare Krishna

My Sweet Lord

We continued on, louder and louder, everyone joining in now, taking hands together, weeping, crying, loving, singing, until the energy took us all higher and higher into an ecstatic rhythm of love and the guitars could no longer be heard. We were all standing, hugging, swaying, singing, even the Swami, all caught up in the fever pitch of the moment. This was OUR bhakti moment, born of OUR modern culture, created by our modern icons, to whom the whole planet related and resonated. We went on singing the roof off the temple, high on the ecstasy of our joint co-creation. Fifteen, twenty minutes of this endless chorus, never wanting it to end, until Swami grabbed my microphone and said "Shush". He had to say it a few times but eventually we settled down and he got us quiet, thanking us for our enthusiasm and sending us gently to bed!

Of course we were all high as kites and there was no way any of us were going to bed! So we went to the beach deck and continued, singing, playing in the warm, humid night air, loving this group, this music, this place and the connections that were being formed and nurtured in this tropical paradise.

I seriously doubt that temple has seen anything of such a high vibration before or after! It was a special night that I would never forget and allowed me to see the power of community, music and vision, and my own gift as a host and impresario.

The following Saturday, on our day off, I decided to hop on the ferry and take a walk around Nassau town. Actually I will admit I was craving a piece of fish and a glass of chilled white wine, so I headed straight to the nearest sea-food restaurant and ordered a nice piece of swordfish and a chardonnay.

Aaahhhh! The small pleasures of life! I felt a bit naughty to be going off the yogic rails but what the hell – we only had one more week anyway and I doubted that this minor indulgence would seriously impact my enlightenment!

After lunch I was strolling down the shady main street heading towards the port when someone yelled out, "Hey Julia, wait up!" It was Chris, one of the American guys from the ashram. He ran over to me and gave me a hug.

"Where are you headed?" he asked.

"Over to the shops and the port. I just wanted a bit of a walk around really. Would you like to join me?"

"Sure, thanks. I'm just walking aimlessly myself so I would love some company."

We wandered over to the docks where the large cruise ships came in. There was a line of horses and buggies waiting to pick up the cruise ship passengers and drive them around old Nassau town.
"What do you think, Julia? Shall we do it?"

It was hot and humid and I was tired.

"Looks great! I'm game."

So we hopped into the nearest buggy and asked the driver for a one hour tour of the town.

I looked a little more closely at Chris. He was friendly with Gita and we had chatted a bit here and there but I had not really noticed him much up till then. He was tall, probably about six feet two inches and slender built with the well-defined muscles of an athlete and the educated speech of an intellectual. He had a thick black shock of hair and deep inquiring brown eyes, He was actually very handsome. Why had I not seen this before?

It turned out he was from Chicago, fresh out of college and twenty-three years old. I was over a decade older than he.

But sometimes age is irrelevant. As we rode around Nassau that day, talking easily and laughing readily, I began to feel more and more attracted to him. Our hands would brush against each other and little tingles of excitement would bubble through me. I could feel an energy building between us that was starting to feel very compelling.

"On your left are the government buildings," explained our buggy driver with the charming Bahamian accent, "and on your right, the Court House."

I felt like a queen with this lovely young man at my side in a surrey with a fringe on the top exploring this beautiful tropical island.

"So how are you enjoying the training?" I asked.

"It's going great," said Chris. "I had no idea what yoga was at all before I came here and I thought it just seemed like a great thing to do after gradutation. My body's feeling really good from all the hatha yoga and I love the chanting – really feel it in the heart."

"Me too. I hated it at first but now I'm actually starting to look forward to it."

"But I just got kicked off my karma yoga duty yesterday," said Chris shyly.

"How so? What happened?"

"Well my duties are in the kitchen chopping vegetables and when I came in yesterday I was feeling a bit grumpy and my energy was low. I guess the head chef picked up on that and told me that I could not be in the kitchen while the food was being prepared if I was in a bad mood as that energy would transfer to the food and the whole community would be affected by it. So they asked me to leave until I felt better."

"The vegetables pick up our energy?"

"Yes," said Chris. "While we are chopping they ask us to pour the love in our heart into the food. We can even chant while we chop, or sing happily as that all helps the love transfer into the food which you all then consume."

"I wondered why it all tasted so good! Must be the love!"

"Yes it's odd, but true. Now I have sensitized myself to that I can taste the difference from day to day, eating the same foods and being aware of the energy in which they were created and the mood in the kitchen. So the chef was absolutely right. Yesterday I was in a funk and needed to get out for a bit and clear myself. I went and sat by the ocean and soon felt better so I could go back in and finish my shift."

"Was anything upsetting you?"

"Nothing major. I was just feeling a bit homesick and missing my friends. But that's evaporated now. Especially being here with you today and having fun here in town."

I liked that. I felt a little warm fuzzy dance in my heart.

Our tour ended and Chris took me by the hand and walked me across the road to buy a juice and a pastry.

"My treat" said Chris.

I liked the feel of my hand in his. It felt supportive and loving. I realized I had not felt that for a while.

After our snack it was time to head back to the ferry. He took my hand again to help me on to the boat and once more I felt that surge of excitement travel up my arm into my heart. I looked up at him as the afternoon sun hit his handsome face.

God he's beautiful. So noble, so strong, like a warrior.

That night after chanting, he waited for me at the temple entrance and took my hand again.

"There's something I want to show you," he said, guiding me down the path towards the ocean. My heart leaped with anticipation! I followed him willingly until we ended up on the beach. It was a lovely moonlit night and there was only the gentlest of breezes coming from the sea. The cicadas were chirping their nightly chorus and the waves were lapping gently onto the shore. We walked along the beach, past Club Med and the cheap local hotel next to it and further to the end of the bay where the beach curved round to a point. There was another fancy hotel out on the point and we walked towards it.

The hotel grounds were quiet as most vacationers were in bed by 11:00 p.m. I didn't care that it was late. I was with Chris and this was romantic. I could sleep later. We walked past the pool and round a large palm tree; and there bubbling away in all its glory was a jacuzzi!

"Let's get in!" said Chris, stripping down to his undies.

I took off my trousers and T-shirt and followed him into the steaming hot water. It felt wonderful! Giggling and feeling a bit naughty for sneaking into the hotel like this, I marveled at our luck at finding no-one else there and at Chris for his discovery.

"How did you know this was here?" I asked.

"I took a walk down the beach the other day and explored. I saw this hot tub and thought it would be so fun to come back at night and use it."

"These jets feel great on my sore muscles!"

"Is your back sore? Here, come closer and let me rub it for you."

I didn't need to be asked twice. I sidled closer and he laid his hands on my shoulders. He began to rub and squeeze the tensions of all my botched headstands out of my tired scapula. He was   really good at massage!

81

"Wow Chris, where did you learn to do this?"

"Nowhere. I just enjoy doing it. Lean forward a bit and I'll get your lower back too,"

I was in heaven. He squeezed and rubbed and I felt like putty in his hands.

Then he stopped. Slowly he turned me around and faced me, looking lovingly into my eyes. I gazed back, seeing something familiar, someone dear to my heart, sensing a resonance between us, a shared vibration. He lowered his face towards mine, nuzzling me, rubbing his face on my neck. I stopped breathing as the tension mounted. Then even more slowly, he brushed his lips over mine, testing the temperature, sensing if I was open for more.... which I was.

And, as if in slow motion, right there in that hot tub on Paradise Island beach, Chris Mitchell kissed me good and long and deliciously. Again, and again...

Time stopped. Everything else melted away and there was only these lips, his semi-naked body pressed against mine, the warm water and the gentle night breeze.

Eventually I came up for air.

God that man can kiss!

There's nothing I like more in the world than a great kisser!

We must have stayed in that tub for hours, tongues probing, hands caressing. I lost all track of time and would have stayed till dawn if Chris hadn't have suggested we leave and walk back. We walked slowly, stopping every few feet to kiss again and enjoy the spectacle of the moonlight on the water, Eventually we made it back to the ashram and to tent city. He walked me back to my tent with much gallantry.

"See you tomorrow. Don't forget to set your alarm!" Chris said as we parted.

Sometimes we don't need much sleep. I was high on Chris and our fledgling romance, but also a little confused.

Here I was, three weeks into a separation from my husband and already emeshing with a new man. It felt right to be with Chris, but I also decided I was going to keep some boundaries around how far we went. I was, after all, still officially a married woman.

And the next day, a very tired one.

Have you ever had the experience that you can feel physically tired from lack of sleep but so high and joyful in your being that the tiredness is completely counter-acted?

That Sunday was one of those days for me. Although I still sat at the back during chanting and was far away from Chris in hatha class, I was aware of his presence, excited at the prospect of seeing him again.

Our chance came at breakfast. We took our plates heaped with love-infused healthy food and walked down to the shade tree by the beach to eat. Normally I have a huge appetite and as my friends used to say in college, where most people have a stomach, Julia has a black hole! But today I picked at my food. Something else was nourishing me. Something very satisfying and profound.

We made small talk that belied the energy that was running between us, then brought our dishes to the kitchen and headed back to the beach again. We still had a little time before the next class so walked to the rocks away from any view from the ashram and as soon as we were out of sight, started to kiss, hungrily, happily, passionately. My own passion surprised me. After the first couple of years of marriage, I had stopped kissing my husband. We made love, but somehow avoided the kissing bit, which to me is more intimate than sex. I realized how much I had missed it. I missed being adored in this way, being caressed, touched, appreciated. The part of me that was woman had been shut down and now she was reawakening in the arms of this beautiful, sensitive, young man who was like a walking open heart. His affections felt pure though, not greedy. I knew I excited him but I felt safe enough to tell him my situation, explain my boundaries and know they would be respected.

The Bhavagad Gita was beckoning. We headed back to class and sat down together, still basking in the delicious vibrations of love running between us.

From that day on we were inseparable. I felt an invisible cord connecting me with him at all times. It tugged on me, drawing me to him, allowing me to feel him even if we were not in the same physical space. I still slept in my own tent – Swami would have frowned on anything other – but began to visit Chris in his tent during our free time. It was wonderful to have intimate time together and allow ourselves to express more fully our feelings about each other. Yet we were both aware of our container - the ashram rules of celibacy and my own self-imposed boundary of no sex until I was officially divorced.

There was something lovely about that though, something innocent, playful and true. The passionate sexual energy had to go somewhere so it exploded out of our hearts. I was falling madly in love with him and he with me. And the feeling of that was pure magic. We could not think of a future, we shared no past; we were just fully alive, present, sensitized and experiencing love here and now on this beautiful island.

The container we were in added another dimension to our connection. The structure of the program made the free time we spent together sweeter, precious, enlivening. We avoided the temptation to talk too much about our history, keeping it brief and to the point, and instead focused on how we were doing right now in present time, sharing our hearts desires and feelings in the moment.

It was beautiful. Time stretched long, like a rubber band and we had a week that seemed to last forever. When I am in love, I feel like I am walking on air; everything is glorious, nothing matters, life looks rosy and lovely. Even the dullest of Bhavagad Gita classes became full of that loving essence that permeated the air between Chris and I. I didn't care what I was doing or where I was. As long as he was nearby, my heart glowed and expanded as though it may suddenly burst into a thousand colors. The "rose-colored glasses" of love became my filter. I could feel nothing but joy and see nothing but goodness in everyone and everything.

Our classes continued and in hatha yoga morning sessions we moved on to more complex breathing techniques and postures. In the afternoons, we played "teacher" for each other in small groups and I got to hone my skills as a communicator of yogic principles, alignment and form. I loved it. I had inherited a loud, booming voice from my Mother, who was a trained opera singer. In the past, my "big mouth" had often got me into trouble when someone heard a comment not meant for their ears. But finally "the voice" had found its niche. It could be both commanding, yet also soft and soothing, helping students to trust and open to my instruction. Teaching felt natural to me and I got positive feedback as a strong, fluid communicator, passing the class with flying colors.

For the other classes, we had a written test to see if we had taken in the essence of the teachings. I hadn't done an examination since I was in college over ten years ago, and was quite nervous to see how I would fare. I need not have worried. The test was relatively simple and on our last Friday evening session in the temple, it was announced that everyone had passed! Teacher training was over!

We had a graduation ceremony on the Saturday when each of us in turn went up to Swami and was given our certificate, with a Sanskrit name that best suited us written on the back of the paper. Mine was "prema". It simply means 'love'; a state that suited me down to the ground at that moment in time. Free from the constraints of my past, stimulated by this beautiful man, Chris, I had blossomed fully into the loving essence that I am, that we all are. It had not escaped the eagle eyes of Swami!

That Saturday night, I did not sleep a wink. I stayed in Chris' tent that night, listening to the Club Med disco, the sound of his gentle breathing and the muffled snores coming from other nearby tents. Waves of bliss washed over me, as I lay in his arms, merging my energies with his, ecstatically happy to just be lying there with him, nothing else needed, only his masculine presence and the love we shared.

But all good things come to an end.

On Sunday March 5th, after our graduation from the training was complete, the moment came when I had to walk down to the dock, backpack stuffed with dirty clothes, ready to board the little ferry boat that would take me back to Nassau and the airport.

Alone.

I will never forget that moment. Swami was there to see us off. I had to pry myself away from Chris, crying uncontrollably and with great compassion Swami started to chant...

'Om Tryambakam

Yajamahe

Sugandim

Pushtivardanam'

"This is your chant for protection while you travel," said Swami. "When you chant this three times, Swami Sivananda will hear you and come to protect you."

I chanted too, with bleary eyes, and have continued to use this chant every time I sit in a boat or a plane, feeling the loving presence of the smiling bald Swami come to my side when summoned, helping me feel safe and secure.

But here I was now, stepping into the boat, miserable, ecstatic, full, empty... "Parting is such sweet sorrow," as Noel Coward once wrote. Sweet, desperate sorrow, heart blasted wide open with such love, such pain.

The next two hours were a blur of tears and movement. My next memory was sitting on the floor in Miami airport feeling numb, vacant. Back in the good ol' USA, heading home to an unknown future, a mess to clean up. I had stepped off the regular planet for a month, got my Self back, opened my heart and regenerated the body. But now I had to go home and face the music, pay the piper, deal with some harsh realities.

Still, I would never be the same. I now felt deeply that my path in life was that of the yogi. I was excited to start teaching, sharing the wisdom and the practices that had so benefited me. I had a new direction and clarity that would propel me forwards, a foundational practice on which I could rely to keep me grounded and open despite any challenges that could and would arise.

****

"Did you ever see Chris again?" asked Bob, scraping the last bite of flan off the plate.
"Yes I did actually – but not until many years later. We both had our own separate paths to tread and when we did connect again, he was in a relationship with someone else so once again we were fated not to be lovers. We are still in touch to this day and he lives on the East coast."

"But the Sivananda yoga style is not what you teach today. How did your yoga evolve into this unique slow flowing style that you currently share?"

"I got thrown another curve ball and had to head to the hills for a while. But for that story we will have to go back to Harbin Hot Springs," I said.

"What do you say we head over to *Los Gringos* bar for a nightcap and I'll fill you in?"

We paid for our flan and wandered out into the still, balmy night air. *Los Gringos* was right across the street and I ordered a Baileys on ice and settled into a cozy armchair, starting to think about how to answer Bob's question.

Chapter 7

Dateline: April 5th 1993
California

My heart sank as I heard the clack of the mailbox. I knew what was in it - bills, bills and more bills. And my ability to pay them was diminishing fast along with my declining credit score and bank balance. I snuggled down deeper inside my cozy comforter, reluctant to get out of bed. Besides, I was not alone there. The top of the comforter was vibrating – Cleo, my orange and white cat had realized I was awake and was starting to purr loudly. I instinctively reached out one hand to pet her, grateful for her companionship and comforting presence.

Raindrops pelted the windowpanes and outside the trees whined with wind. It was one of those wet, blustery spring mornings and I had no work lined up that day to keep me occupied. After returning from the Bahamas, I had gone back to my old standby, massage, but customers were still few and far between and I was struggling to pay my own basic expenses, let alone bills from the other Real Estate we owned. Here and there, I took odd jobs friends would throw my way, but I had to face facts – I was not making it. Something had to change.

The Real Estate market was tanking and we owed more on our investment properties than they were worth. Rental income was down and it just no longer made any sense to hold on to the properties. They would all have to go. The weight of my attachment to them still felt like a lead balloon attached to my forehead, creating a constant pressure, a feeling of walking around in a fog. At some future time, the balloon would burst and my head would explode open. I was not yet   at that point.

****

A few weeks ago, I had moved out of the fancy investment house that Tony and I had purchased two years prior when the market was high, and back into the original tiny three -bedroom bungalow on Ball Way that we had bought when we first married. I'd had to paint and clean after the renters left, but now the place was looking spiffy again. It was home and familiar and not a bad place to lick my wounds and figure out what to do next.

Miao!

Cleo was getting hungry and ready for her breakfast. She started to lick my face with her rough little tongue, her favorite "get Julia out of bed" strategy.

OK OK Cleo. I'll get up.

But I didn't feel like it. I wanted to just pull the covers back over my head and go back to sleep and wake up to find I'd won the lottery and prince charming was on the doorstep to hand me my check. Getting vertical meant the return of the fog and the sense of helplessness and despair that seems to come with the territory of too much debt and a pending divorce.

I fed Cleo, then glumly walked outside into the rain to collect the mail. Sure enough, VISA bills, utility bills for some of our properties and a Macy's' charge card bill. But something else was there that day – a Harbin Quarterly!

The wonderful folks over at Harbin Hot Springs produce a magazine each quarter that lists all their upcoming courses. Knowing I would soon be through with Real Estate and sensing I needed more strings to my bow as a healer, I thumbed through to see what courses were on offer.

To my astonishment, on one of the pages I recognized one of the teachers! The smiling face in the picture with blond, curly hair was none other than Sarah Stewart, one the ladies who used to come to my t'ai chi classes on the beach back in Yelapa at the time I met Tony! She was offering a course called, "Alchemical Hypnotherapy - Rebirthing, Redeathing and Repossession."

I believe co-incidences are Divine signposts. When I feel a tingle go through my body, it is added confirmation that grand forces larger than myself are trying to get my attention! It was crystal clear to me on that cold April day that I was meant to do this course with Sarah and as luck would have it, I had just enough credit left on my VISA card to swing the fee. I had no idea what the course would be about – it sounded a little dramatic – but I felt sure it would add to my arsenal of helpful healing tools.

Besides, I would be escaping the stresses of blocked toilets, angry tenants and pestering debt collectors. I would be back at Harbin, soaking in warm water, hiking forested trails and eating great food. I could use some laid-back hippy energy right about now. Yes. This was where I should go.

****

Two weeks later found me parking my car in the lot below the Meadow Building at Harbin where workshops are held, excitedly grabbing my bags and sleeping gear out of the trunk. I took a deep breath of the fresh mountain air, sniffing the faint, familiar scent of the manzanita trees that dotted the Harbin landscape. A deer and her two fawns watched me with vague interest. The deer are so tame at Harbin you can even hand feed them. But these did not approach me like some of the braver ones – their doe eyes met mine, blinked, then they ran off over the meadow to seek out new pastures.

Still the moment was rich and full. I felt a surge of excitement... maybe it was the encounter with the deer, or maybe, just maybe, I knew that I was walking not only towards the Meadow building, but also towards…(drum-roll)… a date with destiny!

Destiny came in the form of the most brilliant blue eyes

90

I had ever seen. Their owner was tall, slender, with a shock of thick, wavy dark hair and a cowboy mustache. I admit I didn't much care for the mustache, but the kind face it belonged to helped me to see past it. We stared at each other for a moment too long in the Meadow Building kitchen, beside the shelf where the red drinking cups are kept – and for that instant, time stood still. Something indefinable passed between us- then normal life resumed again. He walked into the workshop room and I continued on my way to the bathroom.

It turned out that Mr. Blue Eyes' name was Dale and he hailed from Fortuna, in Humboldt County, Northern California. He was there to assist Sarah for the first couple of days, having completed her course a year ago himself. He could only stay a short while as he had just opened a brand new and very small health food store and healing center back in Fortuna and needed to get back to manage it. Before that, he had been a UPS driver. Now with this recent transition to working full-time in the Healing Arts with bodywork, hypnotherapy and a health food store, Dale was keen to make a success of his new venture.

The next few days were a whirlwind of new learning as Sarah Stewart revealed sides of herself that I had never seen in Yelapa. She was a lively lady of diminutive stature and curly blond hair, around fifty, with a sweet, maternal energy that people instantly trusted and a soothing voice that lulled us all into light trance states whenever she spoke, She was incredibly intuitive at sleuthing out peoples' deepest issues and picking exactly the right person for each demonstration. I watched in amazement as she taught us how to get the body into a state of deep relaxation, then take the person back in time to discover the origin of whatever ailed them.

One lady had suffered with neck pain for most of her life. When Sarah had her go to the source of it, she dropped right back into a past life situation, where she was a young girl in France about to face the guillotine. She described the scene in gory detail. It sounded just like the movies we see of 17th century France with crowds of people watching the

91

unfortunate few lining up to have their heads chopped off. She got up to the point of death, then described the incredible peace that followed as she floated back to the spirit world.

Sarah then performed what she terms as "redeathing." She asked the lady, still in trance, to describe how she would have preferred to have lived that life and how she would have chosen to die. The unconscious mind does not seem to know the difference between the imagined state and the real event, so once a new sequence of imagined events are placed in that time slot from the past, very often, any trauma associated with the original event will disappear and the cellular memory that holds it in place will let go too, healing the body.

The former French lady went on to describe a lovely life full of happy children and marriage, ending in a graceful aging process that culminated with her heart stopping in her own bed surrounded by loved ones. Ahhh. She breathed this new happy thought deep into her cells, filling them with light. Those of us watching could all feel her peace. At the end of the session, when she came back into waking awareness, Sarah asked how her neck felt.

"My God – it feels great! The pain has gone!"

To my knowledge, it never came back.

There is a school of thought that says that many of our personality quirks and phobias begin in the womb. This seemed to be the case with many of us as we took each other back into the birth experience and before to see what might have occurred. One lady had always had the sense of being the odd one out, a social misfit, unwanted. It turned out that in the womb she heard her Mother say to her doctor that she did not want this baby. It was going to be a nuisance and did not fit into her life plan and how could she get rid of it? The doctor was heard to talk her out of an abortion but the trauma of being unwanted registered in the fetus' awareness. The lady started to cry on the table.

"Oh my God – my Mother didn't want me! No wonder I never felt bonded with her or truly loved. For years I felt like she just put up with me."

Her therapist took her through a healing with the spirit of her Mother, where she got to speak her true feelings to her Mother about how she felt growing up. The spirit of the Mother had her say too, and through this magical process, the lady came to a better understanding of her Mother and learned to have more compassion for herself. She comforted her inner child and learned ways of tending to that part of herself, should the feeling of being left out arise in the future.

The weirdest aspect of the work though was 'repossession'. Sarah reckons that a large percentage of our population are possessed by disincarnate spirits and don't even know it! It can explain sudden changes in behavior, addictions or even illnesses. It appears that sometimes someone dies and does not move on up the tunnel of light, as they should. Instead, for reasons of their own, they stay earth-bound. That explains ghost sightings and the like, but in this case, what happens is that the spirit attaches itself to the body of a living person and feeds off their energy. They do not belong there and need to be encouraged to leave. We learned techniques to do just that.

Surprisingly, I found that I was a natural at this. If someone was carrying around an entity, I was really good at getting them to talk to me and trust me enough to tell me what they were up to. Very often, when we made contact, the voice of the person in trance would change quite dramatically and they would use different idioms and accents. It was clear that a completely different persona was speaking.

One day I did a session with June and contacted a male entity called Stan who had been gay in his last life. Stan had also been raised a Catholic, so when he died, he was terrified of moving on from the earth plane as he thought he was going to burn in hell for eternity. He had attached himself to this nice young woman as he sensed she was kind and compassionate and would not judge his past behavior. Besides, June was a frequent visitor to Harbin and he liked it there.

It took a bit of convincing, but I got Stan to admit that he could not stay with June forever and that if I were to go and call a couple of healer angels down from heaven to help him move smoothly up into the next world, then maybe he would feel safe enough to go with them. Reluctantly he agreed. I called on the angelic realms for help and June described seeing angels clearly coming to fetch Stan. She waved him good-bye as he floated up with them to the heavenly realms… and he was gone.

Afterwards June said she felt lighter, much more energized. I was frankly astounded.

You mean I actually performed an exorcism? Such a thing is real and can affect us?

Yet it seems that it can and does. I wondered how many patients in mental institutions just need a good old-fashioned exorcism to clear their haunted minds? It was fascinating stuff and I spent lots of time between sessions talking to Dale about his experience in this strange new world I had discovered.

It was tricky getting Dale to open up. He was a quiet, reserved person of few words. When he did speak, I found myself hanging on to his every utterance as though it were holy, admiring his considered, thoughtful responses and the deadpan way he would talk about the extra-ordinary.

It was clear we had an attraction, although both of us were too shy at that point to act on it. A few days later when he left, he rather awkwardly gave me his telephone number and told me that if I ever got up his way, to please be in touch. I took his number politely and stuffed the piece of paper in my wallet, but as I'd never been that far north in California before, I considered it unlikely. After all, Fortuna was five hours drive away from Sacramento.

Fate had other ideas.

Not even three weeks after Sarah's course, I was sitting at home watching Oprah one afternoon when the phone rang. It was Christie, a close friend of mine, calling to see if I wanted to join her on a family camping trip – to Fortuna!

Goosebumps spontaneously erupted on my arms as she spoke those words and I heard myself agreeing to go with her. I was taken aback at the coincidence of this location appearing twice on my radar screen in so short a space of time and felt compelled to go and find out why.

Fortuna is located in the redwood area of Northern California. The forests are pristine and beautiful, teeming with wildlife and ideal for camping. The following weekend, Christie and I and her two kids made the drive north and found the camping area she had heard was so lovely by the river. We pitched our tents in a shady spot and enjoyed ourselves seeking out the best swimming holes and the prettiest hikes through the forest.

Over the course of that weekend, I plucked up the courage to pick up the pay phone and call Dale. (no cell phones in those days...)

My heart leaped when he answered....

"Surprise! This is Julia from Harbin! Guess what? I'm at the campground five miles down the road from you!"

"I'll be there in ten minutes."

Oh my gosh! Dale is coming to get me!

Just a few minutes later, I saw his truck approach through the tall trees and my heart skipped a beat. I felt that familiar tingle of excitement, where mystery meets unknown future.

The first thing I noticed was that Dale had shaved his mustache off. In my opinion, he looked ten times more handsome, more available. That was good. We greeted each other and I quickly leaped into the passenger seat, eager to leave before Christie's kids engaged Dale in a lengthy show and tell of all their forest discoveries. He whisked me away back to his house in the small hamlet of Hydesville.

Dale's house was a compact bungalow on a hill overlooking rolling fields. I walked in through the front door and came face-to-face with a big, furry stag head! It

95

was mounted on the living room wall surrounded by a gun collection. I looked at Dale quizzically, after all, this was a little incongruous a display for a healer, I thought to myself, especially as he was also a vegan, meaning he ate no animal flesh or dairy produce.

"Oh and don't mind the guns and animals. My Dad is a cowboy and he and I used to hunt. These are mostly his."

A real cowboy? Who ropes and lassoes? How.... American!

I put my purse on the kitchen table, noticing that the counter was packed with bottles – more different kinds of vitamins and herbs than I had ever heard of! Dale was learning the health food business and when I asked what they were all for, he explained he was experimenting on his own body with the effects of nutritional supplements. He picked up a couple of bottles.

"Glucosamine is really helping my joints and large doses of vitamin C have kept me cold-free all summer."

How interesting, I thought. This was a subject I knew nothing about, but natural health fascinated me and I had the sense I could learn a lot from him.

We continued our tour of the house.

His small bedroom had a rich purple quilt on the bed and neatly folded clothes were laid out on a chair. It looked inviting...but before you go in your heads where I think you are going, dear reader, let me tell you something. I was still not officially divorced at that time and even though Dale and I had a strong attraction for each other, we made a pact that very day to keep the brakes on until my divorce became final. It just felt like the right thing to do.

The upshot was, we developed a friendship. We shared an interest in health and healing and had both studied the same type of barefoot shiatsu. That first day at his house, we traded massages and techniques. It felt wonderful. I had studied shiatsu in London originally then later at Harbin but rarely did I find someone to practice with. We spent the afternoon together playing with our bodies, opening our meridians and energy centers, then relaxing deeply together in states of sweet surrender.

The sun started to set and I began to feel guilty at being gone from the campground for so long. I hated to leave Dale, but could not abandon Christie and her family completely, so he dropped me back off at the campground just in time for a campfire supper and we agreed to stay in touch.

After Christie and I returned to Sacramento, Dale and I continued a phone relationship and made plans to see each other whenever one of us could make the five-hour drive. It was a difficult summer for me, wrapping up the Real Estate businesses and proceeding with divorce plans, so I was actually quite happy to make the long drive north and leave my troubles behind as often as I could. The developing relationship with Dale was my saving grace, a lifeline of sanity and love that gave me strength at this challenging time.

When I was up in Fortuna, we would spend our free time in the woods walking amongst the tall trees, talking about mystical things, psychic phenomena and the unexplained. Dale knew a lot about all that, having quite the psychic gift himself and I lapped it all up.

He would have me come and help in his health food store, teaching me about supplements and their healing properties. I helped him stock shelves and serve customers. I had never worked in a store before and found I quite enjoyed it, especially as I got to learn about a subject that interested me while I was there. Driving back to Sacramento at the end of a visit was hard, yet I would leave with a full feeling in my heart, buoyed up and strengthened to deal with whatever was awaiting my return to the city,

One day, Dale called me with barely concealed excitement in his voice....

"I met someone interesting today. His name is Harry. He just walked into my store and after a brief conversation told me to come down and study yoga with him at his center in Garberville. There's something about this guy I'm curious

97

about. So I'm going tomorrow."

I rarely heard Dale over-excited so I paid attention and was curious how it would go.

Two days later, the phone rang again and an even more excited Dale could hardly contain himself.

"I've just had an amazing experience with this guy Harry! You MUST meet him! I've already told him about you. I fell into a state of indescribable bliss in his beginner yoga class. All we did was lie on the floor and do some simple side bends, but the energy he held was so incredible, my mind stopped and I felt like I expanded into infinity and beyond!"

Wow. Infinity and bliss. Sign me up!

Dale was not normally one to be over-enthused about much, so coming from him, this was really something.

He continued, "This guy is the real deal, a proper yogi, not a mere "yoga teacher." His practice is his life, his passion, his path to God. And it shows."

And so, a couple of weeks later, on 10.00am one Wednesday morning, Dale and I drove into the small town of Garberville, Humboldt County and found a parking spot next to The Dharma Center where classes were held. On the wall outside, I noticed a sign saying "Standing Wave Yoga - Hatha yoga for opening the body and Jnana yoga for opening the mind." Times were listed below. We followed a very skinny, young hippy guy up steep, musty-smelling stairs. There was a door on the left with the same poster affixed.

I followed Dale and the young hippy guy into a large carpeted hall with imposing Tibetan *thankas* on the walls and a beautiful altar space at the front adorned with all manner of Buddhist paraphernalia. I guessed the local Buddhist group also used the facility. There was a buzz of excitement palpable in the hall and as I looked around to see what or who was the cause of all the fuss, I came face to face for the first time in this life with Harry the bearded yogi.

He was a large man, muscular and hairy all over. He had long hair almost down to his waist, a long gray beard and long fingernails. And he was wearing a skirt "to remind him of his feminine side." I noticed the incredible intensity of his eyes, their clarity and piercing gaze. All in all, I was a little surprised at his odd appearance – and then I heard him speak... with the thickest Philadelphia accent you have ever heard, booming and gravelly! To be honest, he was a little scary.

When I'm feeling nervous, I tend to say stupid things. Out of my mouth came,

"Hi Harry. I'm Julia and I'm a yoga teacher too. I thought I might come here and pick up a few tips."

Harry sized me up, chuckled to himself and told me to find a spot on the floor. I sensed I had said something stupid and feeling like an idiot, slunk off to the back of the room where I hoped I would not be spotted.

I looked around and started to notice more fully the other students in the Dharma Hall. They looked pretty hippy-like to me – like they could have fit in well at Harbin. Most of the guys had long hair and some of the girls came in wearing big clunky country boots and unfashionable loose pants. Some people wore tie-died shirts. I felt quite out of place. Me, a City girl from London town, up here in the pot-growing capital of the world about to take a yoga class from a guy in a skirt! I looked over at Dale. He was already sitting quietly on the floor and dropping into meditation. No comfort there.

Harry took his place at the front of the class and said, "If you'll please come into a comfortable sitting position, we can begin."

The class chanted OM three times. Harry led some prayers then said:

"If you'll please come lying down on your backs in sivasana, we will begin our breath practice. Legs are splayed outwards, about 12 –18 inches apart. Arms are down by your sides, palms turned up.

Feel the effect of gravity pulling down into the earth and allow the earth to support you. Let go, let go, let go."

At the Sivananda school we had learned some specific breathing techniques, but here we focused on the deep, diaphragmatic breath, spending the first twenty minutes of class only breathing.

Harry came and stood over me, watching, a looming presence that made me feel uncomfortable and self-conscious, wanting to please the teacher but not sure how.

"Bring the breath more fully into the belly, Julia. Yes that's it. Now expand your ribcage out to the sides and draw the breath up to the top of your lungs. Keep your eyes closed. Stay focused within. And relax your face, no grimacing in this class!"

I must have eventually breathed to Harry's satisfaction, because I felt his presence leave and move elsewhere. I had never breathed so hard and deep for so long. I started to feel light-headed, as though I was dissolving. It reminded me of my re-birthing experience, but here the slowness of the breath kept me in control and staved off the temptation to float off into the ether. Well, I did float off a little...going "unconscious" for a few minutes, until something in Harry's voice pulled me back into my body.

Slowly, with much care and attention, we added physical movement to the breath. And in this heightened state of awareness, each simple posture felt ecstatic, expansive, blissful.

Dale was right. There WAS something special going on here. I had never felt that kind of energy before during a yoga class (or since) – like being engulfed by a warm fog of love, the air in the room literally thick with the essence of whatever Divine substance was channeling through Harry.

At the end of the class, I had a hard time coming back from Sivasana, the final resting position, so far away had I drifted from the usual waking state. When I did return, the world looked different – brighter, sharper colors, energized.

I felt light and full – and quiet. I didn't feel like talking much.

In the car going home, Dale stroked my hand as we sat in a full, comfortable silence together. Nothing needed to be said. We both knew we had found our teacher, our yogi – and from now on, wild horses would not keep us away.

Chapter 8

Dateline October 22nd 1993
Yogic Training

"Take off all your clothes and face the back wall so I can get a look at you."

Obediently, I complied with Harry's request. After all, I had given him permission to "disturb my peace" as part of my personal yogic training. It was my first private session with Harry and I was both excited and nervous. I stared awkwardly at the crack in the window of the Dharma Center and my body shivered as clothes dropped in a heap on the floor. I became painfully aware of all my physical flaws, feeling extremely self-conscious as male eyes scrutinized me as never before. *Was my tummy bloated? Was I standing up straight? Were my breasts sagging? What did he think of me anyway?*

The laser-like pierce of his gaze penetrated deeply and he was silent for a while.

Oh God – what is he seeing?

He may have only looked at me for a couple of minutes, but standing there naked in the chilly hall it felt like eternity.

"Your left hip is slightly higher than your right, which tells me that your spine is out of alignment. And there is the start of a scoliosis in your upper back. Don't worry, a few months more of yoga will fix that. Your neck is probably out too – lie down and I'll take a look."

I dutifully lay on the mat, hoping to God that he knew what he was doing. I had had a car accident years ago and my neck was often out of alignment and sore. Harry knelt down at my head, his looming masculine presence engulfing me. He smelled faintly of Chinese herbs and incense. Strong, hairy hands felt around my neck, twisting, turning, prodding the soft flesh.

"Take a deep breath in and as you exhale, relax."

Crack! He snapped my neck back into place. My neck felt instantly better and I could feel my back muscles releasing now that the vertebra were aligned.

"OK you can put your clothes back on. Now sit down and tell me about what's going on in your life."

The tears rolled down my face as I related my sad tale of divorce, bankruptcy, foreclosure and homelessness. At least I did have a roof over my head – Dale's roof. After I lost all the properties, he had kindly offered to take me in. I had stuffed my furniture in storage and driven north; some clothes, Cleo, the cat and me. Dale wasn't that happy at having the cat in his house as he is severely allergic to cats, but I wasn't leaving my trusty companion, so we had made a little bed for her in the utility room and I could play with her outside. She seemed to love the large field in front of the house and amused herself hunting for voles and mice, her city life soon forgotten.

Now that I was living in Humboldt County full-time, I could study more seriously with Harry. He offered classes and private sessions three days a week, Tuesdays through Thursdays, and I drove down to all of them, the hatha yoga classes, the meditation class and jnana yoga group. After class one day, when Harry announced he was open to taking a few more students for private yogic training, I had timidly raised my hand and asked to be included.

And here I was, blabbing my eyes out in front of the bearded one.

"Listen Julia. It is no coincidence you are sitting here. You and I have done this dance together many times before, except that sometimes it's you who are sitting at the front of the class, not me."

Goosebumps appeared on my skin.

Is he talking about past lives? I assumed he was... I had no recollection of any of that, but it seemed that he did. I was surprised, to say the least.

"The timing is appropriate too. Life has beaten you up some. Now you are teachable. You have a stubborn nature and I doubt you would have been open to these teachings before now. So here we are...."

I have to admit, Harry was probably right. My t'ai chi teacher in London had said I was the most impatient student he had ever met. Like my Mother, I wanted to do everything quickly. I had a quick mind; I spoke fast and learned fast, but sometimes not thoroughly. Harry would never stand for that. He had nailed me on my speediness right off the bat and was going to do his darnedest to cure me of that tendency.

After my second class with him, he had said,

"You will spend the next six months in beginner class, Julia. If you learn how to breathe consciously, I will consider allowing you to try the intermediate class."

My heart had sunk.

Six months more of lying on my back?

That had sounded very dull. But there was no arguing with Harry. It was his way or the bye-way.

But he had been right. Now I could see the wisdom of that demand. In the six months repeating the beginner class time and time again, I had expanded my capacity to breathe fully and deeply and had managed to move slowly and consciously enough to finally gain Harry's approval. Next week I was going to be able to try the intermediate class. Oh what excitement! And here I was, one of the few to be doing private work with him.

"I am going to give you a couple of practices that will help clear out some of the energy you are carrying from your marriage," said Harry.

"First is a practice to release anger. For thirty days, one minute a day, you will move and scream uncontrollably. If

104

you skip a day, you must go back to day one and begin the thirty-day count again. Now let me watch you do it."

Self-consciously I stood up and started to pound my fists in the air, yelling – a bit.

"More Julia, give it up! Let yourself go! Open up those powerful lungs of yours and shout out all the pain and frustration you've been feeling these past few months."

Well OK then. I opened my mouth and let a scream rip… as if I were having a "temper tantrum."

It was exhausting, and hard to even manage a minute, but afterwards, I felt cleansed, lighter. I could do this!

"The second practice is to get you re-connected with nature, which will help to heal your emotional body. Twice a week I want you to go and sit somewhere quiet outside and open your senses to your surroundings. First, look up at the sky. Taste the sky, hear the sky, smell the sky and touch the sky. Then look at a tree in the distance and do the same. Then a nearby bush. Finally, the ground beneath you. Tune in....get out of your head and have an experience. You do not KNOW how to do this. It does not make sense to your mind. That's the point. Keep the intention strong and use your witness consciousness to notice what arises. Next time I see you, I want a full report."

The hour was soon up and I trotted off down the stairs with a warm glow in my heart. I felt supported, loved by this big, hairy man. Instinctively I knew he had my best interests at heart, even though he could be harsh and scary.

At the foot of the stairway outside the corridor, Dale was waiting. He had taken the day off work and driven down with me. He normally managed to come at least once every week, making the yoga practice a priority and commitment in his life as much as work at the new health food store would allow.

"So how did it go?"

"OK I suppose. He had me strip naked and cast his eye over me pretty thoroughly. That was a bit disconcerting.

But I have practices to do and next week I get to go back and give my full report. It's a bit like being back at school, but a life school. These are skills I could never have learned anywhere else."

Dale took my hand and led me to the car. We were trying to make a go of our romance, but to be honest, it was not going swimmingly. Dale had been a bachelor for many years and now he had me in his living space. It had changed the energy between us and although I tried to fit in to his household, I kept doing things that upset him. The other day it was raining and I had let Cleo into the living room. She was so happy to be inside on my lap and we purred together for a couple of relaxing hours watching the raindrops patter against the window.

But Dale had come home and started to sneeze the moment he walked in the door. "Did you let that cat in here?"

I couldn't lie.

"Just for a little while. It was raining. Plus I was feeling lonely and really needed her company."

I sensed his anger and tried to placate him, but he just scowled at me and walked away, making me feel quite uncomfortable.

I knew it had been a stretch for him to let me move in. If it had not been for the dire straits in which I found myself, we would both have preferred I live elsewhere. But I was broke, exhausted and at my wits end. I had suggested that I could help him in the store a few days a week in exchange for rent and food and that was a good arrangement for us both. Plus we were able to put our compatibility to the test.

It was soon clear that we were not. I am a city girl, he had been raised a cowboy in the country. I tried his vegan diet for a while until my hair started to fall out and I became severely anemic. My diet needed more animal protein, but Dale was disgusted at the thought of eating meat. I liked to be social and hang out with friends, he was a solitary loner.

106

Despite our differences, I stayed nine months with him in his house; nine months in which to recover my energy, heal my emotional pain from the divorce and study the yoga. And looking back, that was really why I was there, to be with Harry and immerse on the Standing Wave Yoga.

****

Harry was a genius.

Years ago, he had been a high-flying shoe-salesman on the East coast. He wore fine clothes, Italian shoes and had a large, comfortable home complete with wife and her kids. He also had a bad back. He had tried yoga and was surprised how much better he felt after practice. But the type of practices he was doing, whilst beneficial, were not actually healing his back problem.

One day, lying in pain on the bedroom floor, Harry felt desperate. He said aloud, "If there is a God, and you are listening, teach me how to heal this back. If you do, I promise I will devote my life to sharing the tools you give me."

He heard a voice saying, " Well, now that I have your attention, we can begin."

And with that, the 'floor series' channeled through him, a masterful, simple set of hatha yoga movements all done on the back along with deep, diaphragmatic breathing.

After eighteen months, Harry noticed that his back no longer hurt him. He resigned from his job, told his wife he was moving on, and walked out leaving all his possessions to her; no fuss, no wrangling, just exit stage left.

He came to California with the shirt on his back and little else and started to teach. As he did, more sequences came through. His genius was in breaking the regular hatha yoga poses down into micro-movements to get us, the students, conscious of all the components. For example, we would spend forty-five minutes building the individual pieces of triangle pose or pigeon pose so that when we actually did come into the full posture, the effect was completely different than coming in cold without the benefits of the warm-ups. It also moved a helluva lot of energy. We would be groaning and moaning out the issues in our tissues. It was a noisy class!

"We feel the issues going in and we need to feel them moving out. This is the pain of opening – very different from the pain of injury," Harry would say as we writhed across the floor. " And we accept all of it. This is a tantric practice. It's all sacred, including our pain. We embrace it, love it and gentle it out. That way when we die, we offer our God a well-loved being."

Harry's eagle eyes were on all of us as we practiced. He would accept nothing less than a full commitment to practice, to ourselves and to love. If he ever caught us pushing too far we would be reminded to go more gently, more loving.

"The body needs to learn to trust you again. Right now you are contracted in that muscle. It will stay that way until YOU allow it to soften with breath, time and love."

Oh, how great I felt after the effort had been made and I could lie back in final relaxation and absorb the energy that was careening around my system! So much would release from the joints, muscles and soft tissues... and in sivasana (final relaxation pose), I would relax deeply and be carried away into realms of bliss by angels' wings, carefree, melted, ecstatic.

Then there was jnana yoga group. This was the first I had heard of jnana yoga, wisdom yoga – or self-inquiry. We would all sit down in the Dharma hall in a large circle and Harry would ask what was going on for us. Students would raise their hand and talk about an issue or challenge they were going though and Harry would give responses that absolutely amazed me. His comments were so wise, so clear. I listened with bated breath, hanging onto every word, wondering how he could pull such valuable lessons for everyone out of seemingly thin air.

I never raised my hand. That would have been way too

scary. Instead I sat quietly and absorbed it all like a sponge. There would be fifty or sixty students in the hall for jnana, even more than for hatha classes. Some students talked about breakthroughs in awareness, or physical healings.

I wanted a breakthrough.

At that time I felt pretty broken, a failure, powerless. I was sleeping twelve hours a day and had no energy for anything much. I was not capable of full-time work. Helping Dale down at the health food store two or three days a week was about all I could manage.

Then one day something happened.

I was taking a walk in the countryside near Dale's house and had sat down in a pretty green meadow and to do my "nature connection" exercise. It was a lovely, sunny fall day and the birds were singing cheerfully in the clear blue sky as I started to clear my head in preparation for the exercise. I had tasted the metal of the sky, smelt the freshness of the tree on the horizon, heard the subtle rustling of the bush across the field and felt the moistness of the ground beneath me. I had been doing this exercise for a few weeks now and had no idea if I was making any progress with it, but it always felt calming to do it and I loved any excuse to go out for a walk on my own.

After a few minutes of opening my senses in this way, I had gotten up from the meadow and started to walk home along the quiet country road. Suddenly, I heard the sound of clip-clop behind me. I thought it might have been someone riding a horse, so continued to walk on without stopping. But the hoof sounds came closer. I stopped and turned around.

And there, trotting eagerly up the road was a full-grown deer! And he was heading my way! I stood stock-still. It crossed my mind that he was a wild animal and could be dangerous. But what would he want from me? He slowed to a walk, came right up and stopped, gazing at me innocently with those large, brown doe-eyes. It seemed like he wanted me to pet him. So very gently and slowly, I raised my hand to his muzzle and rubbed softly. The deer

109

didn't move. He let me continue to touch him, his neck, his powerful back, and his noble, furry face.

In fact, when I stopped, he pushed his moist nose into my hand so I would continue!

We stood in this animal-human embrace for about twenty minutes. The deer would not go away. It half-occurred to me that maybe it was a tame deer and would trot away to someone's home after its little encounter with me. But no. When eventually I needed to get going and started to walk down the road, the deer bounded off across the meadow and into the forest, to be absorbed once more into the wild.

The following Wednesday, I sat in front of Harry excitedly repeating this miraculous tale, eager for his take on the incident.

"See, Julia, when you connect yourself with the natural world, as you did when you did the exercise, the deer can sense no difference between you and it. He trusts you as an extension of himself. And in that place, he wanted to connect with you, to share a moment of love between species. That was a piece of Grace, but you earned it. Well done."

My heart swelled with pride. Harry had said "Well done!" It was hard to earn his praises and of course, all we students yearned for them, as small children do with their fathers. This training was starting to work. I was feeling better, too. Little by little, my energy was coming back and I was less exhausted, more alive. The fog in my head was clearing.

I had completed my thirty days of anger release and was now practicing being in absolute integrity, sharing my personal truth as it arose, being honest in all transactions and being my word.

"Being your word will do wonders for your self-worth," declared Harry. "But be cautioned – if you are going to give your word and make a commitment, be very careful what you commit to. Take time to think about what really serves you before saying "yes" to just anything. Because once you do commit, you must execute your commitment."

I started to think about my relationship. I had been living with Dale for nine months now and quite honestly, it felt stagnant, going nowhere. It was clear that my truth was, I needed to move on. Nine months, a gestation time, a time of re-birth for me.

It was hard to leave the beauty of the woods and security of life with Dale, but we both agreed it was for the best, for both of us. I left Humboldt County renewed, energized and hopeful for my future and moved back to Sacramento.

And yet I did not leave Harry.

****

I stayed with friends in Sacramento while I got myself some work and after a few months, found a more permanent place to live. I started teaching yoga at Christ Unity Church, my first paid yoga-teaching job and got to know other teachers in the area. But I missed Harry, his amazing energy, his gravelly voice yelling, "Just let it go." It occurred to me that my Sacramento yoga teacher friends would appreciate his teachings as much as I did.

So one April day, I called Harry with a proposal.

"Hi Harry, it's Julia."

"Hello Julia. How's it going in Sacramento?"

"Pretty well, actually. I miss you though. And I've thought of a way that I could see you more, if you're open to it."

"I'm listening..."

"Well I know a lot of people in town and I'm pretty connected to the yoga community here now, so how about I sponsor you to come down and teach classes for a weekend? You could offer a beginner floor series class, an intermediate class and a jnana group. Perhaps you could start with a Friday night introductory talk. My friend, Siri

Gian Singh often hosts groups at his house and he is willing to offer his place for Friday and my other friends, Bill and Sarah, are offering their house and garden for hatha and jnana classes. So as I see it, we have nothing to lose and lots to gain. If you say yes, I'll start marketing down here and assuming there is good interest, all you have to do is show up and teach."

"Alright, Julia. I am willing to come and support your community. Let's try it."

A couple of weeks later, Harry and I were walking up the grand stone steps of Siri Gian's turn-of-the-century midtown house together. I was shaking with excitement! The response had been unbelievable, such was the hunger in our town at that time for spiritual teaching. Plus I had my own testimonial to add, my affirmation that this was a man worth hearing. It was a warm spring night and pigeons cooed in the tall oak trees lining the street. The day had been hot, over ninety degrees, but the house stayed cool thanks to the shade of the ancient trees that graced this part of Sacramento with their shady canopies. It is said that Sacramento has the most trees of any city in the world per square hectare, bar Paris. They lend a charming ambience to the grid pattern of mid-town, that older area of Sacramento built one hundred years ago inside the river curves.

Siri Gian welcomed us as we took off our shoes and went inside. He was my kundalini yoga teacher, a wonderful man with twenty-five years of study with yoga Bhajan behind him. A Sikh, so turbaned and wearing white, Siri Gian was the perfect host, welcoming us into his lovely home, carpeted inside with oriental rugs and completely devoid of furniture. This was a house devoted to yoga; no need for couches or entertainment cabinets here. There were some woolly sheep fleeces to sit on stacked in a chest, a shoe rack, a stereo and precious little else except some tasteful artwork. Lighting was subtle, coming mostly from Christmas fairy lights that were draped around the walls. It gave the room a calming effect, a sense of peace pervading that helped me settle down a bit that April night.

112

Harry placed himself at the front of the room and went into meditation. He had a large brown shawl completely covering his face, so as people came in, all they saw was this shape sitting silently at the end of the room, no telling who was underneath the shawl.

I welcomed the guests; eager, anxious faces, the faces of dear friends I had begged to come, of fellow yoga teachers I respected, of other spiritual seekers who had heard a rumor about a new teacher in town. One by one, they placed their shoes in the rack by the door, grabbed a fleece to sit on and found a spot on the floor. There was a buzz of excitement in the room, the sound of hushed but lively conversation, the sense of expectancy.

Oh God, Harry, you'd better be on tonight. Most of these people are here because of my enthusiasm for you. Don't let me down.

He didn't.

Forty people showed up that night. From the moment Harry opened his mouth to speak, they were riveted. He spoke of loving the self, of opening to trust, of the Divine Mother and her messages to him, of healing and the difference between yoga teachers and being a real yogi. But it wasn't the words that were really important. It was the energy. Some magic dust was in the air that night. The room felt charged, the energy amplified by unseen forces. We were left with the sense of being in the presence of something great, an aftertaste of sweetness, a glow of vibrancy that lingered. Not that it necessarily came from Harry – no, this was something else. It was as though he was an open channel for some unseen force to work through him, a portal for Grace, a conduit for the Divine to reach out and touch us all with the healing wand of love.

There was a stunned silence as he finished speaking. No one moved. We all just sat there, lapping up the energy, hesitant to be the first to break the spell.

Eventually, some people needed to leave and there was movement. Some came over to me to sign up for classes. Some went to see Harry to get a hug or ask a question or simply stare into his eyes. Needless to say, the evening was a huge success. My heart swelled with pride as I watched my hometown community embrace "my yogi." Harry too, was thrilled by the warm reception and was noticeably fired up for his classes that coming weekend.

"The people here are ready for this, Julia, and I am happy to serve them. And you, my dear, are a yogi of community. This is your forte. You are an excellent net- worker and people respond well to your suggestions. I think together we will have a big influence on the energy of this town and on the yoga community here."

Sure enough, a large number of students showed up for classes that weekend and a Sacramento group was quickly established. Monthly visits became the norm and we all looked forward to the weekends when Harry would come down to challenge us all, both in hatha and jnana classes. Plus it drew we fledgling teachers together to form our own community. Yoga was less popular at that time and was not as well known as it is today. We were just a handful of teachers in a town of a million people and sharing a Master teacher like Harry as a community became a glue that held us all together and created many long-term friendships and partnerships.

One month, I took Harry to Harbin with me to rest for a day before he went home. He had never been before and I got to watch him enjoy those amazing warm waters for the first time. They have a yoga program there too so I introduced him to a couple of the teachers and invited them to Sacramento to see him next time he came. Not only did they come en masse to see Harry, which resulted in the Harbin yoga program switching almost exclusively to teach Standing Wave Yoga, but he fell in love with Harbin too and wanted to teach workshops there.

"Let's do a Mother's Day retreat here, Julia. The energy here is SO conducive for practice and the water in the springs very healing. We'll honor the Divine Mother that weekend as others are honoring their birth Mothers."

Thus, the Mother's day retreat tradition started. Harry

114

went every year, his following building more and more.

And yet, he would say, "I'm always looking for a few less students." He was strict and expected us to be on time or we would be locked out of class. We were allowed to mess up one time only and after that, if we were not in class fifteen minutes ahead of everyone else, we were out of the program. No excuses. Not tolerated. 100% commitment to showing up or don't bother to come. I watched as over the years, some students got themselves kicked out. It made me shudder. What if that was me? How could I live without Harry, without the support of the teachings, without the warmth of the yoga community?

As my life re-established itself in Sacramento, I would still drive up to Humboldt once a month and Harry would come to me once a month so we saw each other every two weeks. It worked rather well. Harry valued me as his marketing and promotional person in town and I valued this special position that gave me his ear that allowed me to call him for any reason night or day. He was there for me, personally, as I was there to promote him and the work. He knew I was committed to it and saw in me the one who would most likely have the smarts and ability to spread his work in the future, to teach more widely than he had allowed himself to do.

"You know, Julia, when I lived in LA, Hollywood came knocking. I was offered all kinds of money to make videos of my yoga flows. But I refused them all. I was looking to lose my ego, not aggrandize myself more. I will leave you to be the one to do things of that nature. Your temperament is different to mine. You can handle it with more grace."

Harry was right. It did seem to be my calling to make the videos. They came first. The books came way later. I had immersed myself in his teachings and over time, had started to teach more myself, running my own yoga retreats at Harbin and teaching classes at Sacramento City College as well as at Unity Church. I started to build my own following. It felt so good to teach, so energizing and pure. I would skip home after class feeling terrific, knowing I was

115

helping others to heal as these practices had helped me.

I think Harry was proud of me, as a Father would have been of a daughter. I could not imagine our relationship ending. But one of Harry's favorite sayings was that everything has a beginning, a middle and an end. The trick is knowing which stage you are in and accepting it.

The end came rather rapidly.

It was my seventh year of study with Harry and I had been going up to Humboldt every month for teacher training. One class was about the four pillars of relationship. It was essentially a lecture where we listened and asked questions. For some reason, I had asked Harry a question and he refused to answer me. (No longer timid, I was in the habit of asking plenty of questions now!) He didn't like my question. It was a piercing, pithy question about his personal life that related to our discussion topic and he did not want to answer. But like a dog with its bone, I wouldn't let it go. I kept asking, rephrasing, needling him.

There was an icy silence in the room and other students shifted uneasily in their places. My voice got louder and more forceful and so did his. It became painfully obvious that this was a clash of wills, of strong wills, and that there would be consequences to this interaction. My question still unanswered, at some point I shut up. But inside, I knew it was finished. I had booted myself out of Standing Wave Yoga. There was no public confrontation permitted. You dare to confront Harry, you are out. I knew it and yet a part of me made myself do it anyway. As though choiceless, I acted in a way that I knew meant the end of our relationship.

After class, I went and sat in his lap. There was nothing to say. He cradled me like a baby for a few minutes in his strong, hairy arms, sensing my sadness, but with no need to respond. It was simply time, the end, and we both knew it.

I drove the five hours back to Sacramento crying my eyes out. I never spoke to him or saw him again.

116

****

"And does he still teach?" Bob asked, curious.

"No. I hear that he is retired now and spends most of his time living quietly in the hills. You know, Bob, I feel so privileged to have caught the wave of that energy that came through Harry when he was in his teaching prime and to have learned so much. Not only did I heal myself, but his teachings changed my whole life. I, too, have devoted my time and energy to sharing what I learned, to passing on the miracle of the practices. It's been a huge blessing to me and I cannot imagine my life without it. And of course, he inspired our present day jnana yoga group. Our entire Sacramento community owes its origin to Harry and his work. I am forever grateful."

"Well, me too, then. Being part of the jnana community has been great. Pretty much all the friends I have today I met at group."

I yawned and glanced at my watch.

"Good God, it's after midnight! It's time for this little one to head for bed. Let's get the bill and go back to the hotel. After all, tomorrow we have an early morning flight home."

PART 2

ON FIRE

Chapter 9

Dateline: May 3rd, 2011
Sacramento

"Excuse me, but may I zip you up?"

The lady standing behind me in the line at the post office looked a little sheepish. I was standing at the counter buying stamps and had no idea what she was talking about.

What?" I asked, a little taken aback.

"Your dress has come undone," she whispered.

It was true. The zipper on my dress had come down exposing my bare back for all to see, almost down to my knickers! Taking a deep breath and ignoring the stares and sniggers, I nodded and she kindly rendered me decent. How had I not noticed that I was half naked? I don't know whose turn it was to dress me that morning, but they'd got it wrong, seriously wrong! With as much nonchalance as I could muster, but inwardly wishing the ground would open and swallow me up, I calmly strolled out of the Post Office into the spring sunshine and back to my car as though nothing untoward had occurred.

But something had occurred. Was I just so stuck in my head with a million thoughts that I did not notice my wardrobe malfunction or was I really losing my marbles? Since returning from Cabo, it's seemed like my hormones have dropped beneath some critical amount and changes are happening at a fast and furious pace. The absolute worst thing has been the amount of heat in my body at night. I have been waking up sweating about every half hour, unable to sleep for long, and as a result, have felt irritable

119

and tired during the day. For me, the quality of life is determined by my amount of good sleep. Lack of sleep colors everything, especially my capacity for clear thought.

Perhaps it's therefore not surprising that my mind is not as sharp as it used to be. Twice today I walked into a room and could not remember why I was there! I literally walked around in a circle in my office, looking for clues, unable to find any. Last week I forgot to meet my best friend for lunch. She called me from the restaurant wondering where I was. I have NEVER done that before! It's been a life-long yogic practice for me to be my word, always in integrity. My friends all know I am very reliable – usually; maybe not anymore.

I have also gained weight. Not so much that you would call me a tub of lard exactly, but I have always been trim and seven pounds more on my five foot four inch frame shows. My jeans are uncomfortable to do up and I notice I am avoiding wearing them. When I do a side bend in yoga practice, I am restricted by a roll of fat around my middle parts. My face looks puffy. And the kicker is, I am NOT over-eating!

When I was younger, I ate like a horse. As a student I ate so much one day that my roommate remarked, "Where most people have a stomach, Julia has a black hole." But nowadays I generally eat a healthy organic diet and keep my calorie count low when I am home. This has not changed; but I have. The fact is, my metabolism is slowing down.

Not only that, but I have been feeling flat, unexcited about my life, even though my career is doing really well and I lead a relatively glamorous lifestyle of teaching and travel. I feel like I am stuck in my familiar routines, on cruise control, leading a comfortable life that may be fine for some people but not for me. I feel dull, uninspired; even bored. And definitely not sexy.

I have always been a sensual person, loving massages, hugs and foot rubs, but now the compelling desire for touch appears to have evaporated. Is that what they mean by "men on pause?"

For a few months now I have remained single and have not felt any desperate need to be sexual with anyone, even myself, as would have been the case a couple of years ago. Recently a former lover called and invited me to reconnect and I turned him down. Three years ago, I was crazy about this particular man and would have leaped at the chance to run into his arms. Things have changed. The honest truth was, he lived two hours away and I could not be bothered to drive all that way just for sex, even good sex! In fact, I have not felt attracted to anyone recently. The sizzle appears to have left my sozzle.

After the Post Office incident, I drove home, kicked off my shoes and flopped down on my cozy couch, feeling tired, alone and more than a little shell-shocked.

A REALLY DARK THOUGHT entered my head....

What if I never fall in love again? What if that, too, is a hormonally-based experience that fades away with declining estrogen levels? Connecting with men and opening my heart used to be so easy back in my thirties, but on reflection, it has been literally years since I have fallen head over heels with a man.

Let's see – fuzzy mind, fat, hot, sleep-deprived and dull... a recipe for depression if ever I saw one. No wonder so many middle-aged women turn to Prozac. Luckily for me, I have a yoga practice that helps to keep me open and vibrant and I can hardly imagine trying to deal with this life change without it. But this spring day, I sat collapsed on the couch, unmotivated to move, miserable dark thoughts swirling around in my head.

This was not like me.

When all else fails, it's time to bring out the heavy guns... The Floor.

In times of deepest distress in my life, I have found the floor the best place to be - the carpeted floor in my living room to be exact. I light a candle, put on some hypnotic music and lie down on my back. S*ivasana; c*orpse pose;

playing like dead; the ultimate pose of surrender. I lie here and talk to God, allowing myself my complaints for a full ten minutes or so, and when I have got them all out, I relax again and wait to see what happens. I tune inside and listen, see if my intuition/higher self has anything to tell me. Sometimes it does, sometimes not – but I always feel better afterwards; refreshed, calmer, more at peace.

I rolled myself onto the floor, spread-eagled on my back and closed my eyes. Tired as I was, it felt good to lie and rest, letting go of the outside world and tuning within. I began a conversation with ...whoever it is in the spirit world whose job it is to listen to such things.

"Now listen, this body is having a hard time. I'm exhausted and tetchy and I can't sleep. I can't go on like this.... help me! What the hell am I supposed to do here?"

I lay quietly for a while and waited.

Then I heard Harry's voice in my head...."You have a right to know what is going on in your body."

Of course! It's especially true right now with this hormone challenge! I have a responsibility to understand what is happening so I can make informed decisions! It's time for some research....

3 days later....

I have just read the book "Stay Young and Sexy with Bio-identical Hormone Replacement" by Jonathan Wright and Lane Lenard. What an appealing title! It taught me a LOT about hormones and about the horrors of traditional HRT (hormone replacement therapy). What follows is a summary of the research so painstakingly provided in much detail in that book.

Progesterone and Estrogens decline naturally in women as they age, especially after the age of forty. With that come the symptoms we associate with menopause: hot flashes and night sweats, fuzzy thinking, low libido, dry vagina, wrinkled skin, weight gain, loss of muscle mass, depression, poor sleeping patterns, memory loss.

There is no single hormone called estrogen. It's actually a "group name" for describing estrogen subtypes, the main ones being estrone, estradiol and estriol. Curiously enough, the human body has not been found to contain any horse hormones. Yet that is precisely what doctors have been prescribing women for many years with the drug 'premarin', which is extracted from the urine of pregnant mares. The horses are tethered in tiny spaces to ease collection of their urine and kept dehydrated to increase the potency. This is unnatural and uncomfortable for the animal.

In the late nineties, a study was undertaken by the Women's Health Initiative to evaluate the efficacy and safety of conventional HRT in women after menopause. There had been a significant climb in breast cancer rates for women over forty in the last half of the twentieth century and the study was funded to make sure that HRT was not the cause.

In 2002, the study was abruptly halted. It showed definitively that HRT was far less useful and far more dangerous than most doctors had believed. As the scientific papers were published, prescriptions for HRT plummeted along with a corresponding decline in breast cancer rates. Of course, it cannot be proven that HRT has categorically been the sole cause of cancer in any one individual, but the correlation of the evidence is too strong to be ignored. Hence any doctor with morals and integrity would never dream of prescribing Premarin. It's like saying to a woman, "Here, take this drug and your hot flashes will go away. You may die of cancer within the next five to ten years but at least you'll sleep well in the meantime."

My Mother was one of those statistics. She was one of the lucky ones. After years of using HRT, she developed ovarian cancer, but it was caught early and she had the tumor safely removed, with no further complications. Thank God for the British National Health system.

Needless to say, this has not been good news for Wyeth

123

Corporation, the manufacturer of Premarin. They launched a publicity campaign to persuade doctors that their product was still safe and persuaded the FDA to approve a new lower dosage version of their drug, even though this drug had not been tested and it was only a guess that it might be safer. In fact, recent research has shown that the lower doses do nothing to improve its safety risk.

Before we women all throw up our hands in horror and run for the Prozac, I am excited to tell you the brilliant news that there is now another option... bio-identical hormones. They are derived from the Mexican yam plant, so no poor mares have to be tortured to collect the raw materials. They are molecularly exactly the same as human hormone molecules and as such pose a much lower health risk, according to the research papers in many European and Asian journals.

Admittedly, this is still a relatively young area of research, but so far, it's been found that if the hormones are prescribed correctly by testing the individual woman's hormone levels and using a compound pharmacy to mix up exactly the right formula for her needs, there appears to be little danger and huge benefits. Not just hot flashes, but all of the menopausal symptoms can be reversed.

Who knew? Why has this not been shouted from the rooftops? Well, that's a whole other issue related to the connection between Big Pharma and the FDA and politics and big money people and is beyond the scope of this book to explain. But you get the picture. Big Pharma cannot make money out of a product that is naturally sourced, like a herb or vitamin, so all they can do is to try to block the sale of an alternative to their product. Luckily for us, they have not completely succeeded.

I got on the internet and found some local naturopaths and doctors who prescribe bio-identical hormones. My appointment is made and I am raring to try them! I will report my findings to you soon... stay tuned!

And more great news to cheer me up... my old women's group is going to get together in July! We have not been together for twenty years so this reunion will be really exciting! I can hardly wait to see the ladies and hear what wisdom they can share with me about their own aging process!

Chapter 10

Dateline: July 21 – 23rd, 2011
Women's group

The doorbell rang and excitedly I ran to open up.

"I can't believe I'm here!" screamed Linda!

She gave me the longest, juiciest hug and we grinned at each other from ear to ear.

"Come on in already! How was your flight? Do you need the loo? Can I get you a cup of tea? Are you hungry?"

Words tumbled out as I grabbed her bags and took them to the spare room.

"Yes to all of the above!" She laughed her special Linda laugh as she headed off to find my bathroom.

I felt overjoyed to see her. Linda had been my best friend during my marriage and also my original partner in the retreat business. We concocted our very first weekend together in July 1992 in Lake Tahoe by renting a wonderful house with six bedrooms and inviting friends to come up for the weekend. We charged the grand sum of $125 to cover expenses and did it more for fun than anything else. Our friends all LOVED our program... and Linda's amazing home-cooked food. She was from the East coast originally and used to own a restaurant in New Hampshire that would attract customers from miles around. Being a Mom and housewife had not exactly utilized her talents to their fullest, so cooking on the retreats became a creative outlet for her and certainly helped me launch what was to become my full-time work a few years later.

After her divorce, Linda had ended up moving back East to be with family and eventually re-marrying, this time to her childhood sweetheart from High School. Because of the distance, we had not seen each other for years, hence our huge excitement at this   reunion.

A year or so prior to our first retreat, Linda had introduced me to the women's group. We would meet every two weeks on new moons and full moons and utilized a marvelous book called "Connecting at the Heart," which was full of enriching meditations and exercises. Through the book I was introduced to the chakra system, to guided visualizations and group dynamics. We all took turns leading and it was where I cut my teeth as a group facilitator.

Imagine a time when we lived in tribes. Groups of men and women would cluster together for safety, support and community. Women of the tribe would meet to do women's work, engage in sacred rituals and have a laugh at their men! They would sit in circle and talk, share and tell stories.

In modern times, rituals and circles are mostly gone. Yet many busy women like myself have a deep, unidentified yearning to sit in circle with other women who agree to treat each other and the gathering itself as sacred; to listen whole -heartedly to what each woman has to say, holding her in support and compassion, receiving her in her wholeness without judgment or criticism.

Most of us in the group were married thirty-somethings. Over the years, women came and left the group, but a core of us remained for quite a while, supporting and encouraging each other to be in our truth and speak up for our needs.

The consistency of our gatherings gave stability to my life when things started to unravel in my marriage. Indeed, when things went awry, I found safe sanctuary with my women's group friends. The day I left home for good, it was to one of these ladies that I ran - me, my cat and a whole truckload of my furniture.

Between then and now, many of the women had moved away from Sacramento. Some of us had tried starting groups with other women, but all reports came back the same – there was a synergy with our particular group that was hard to imitate. Other groups just did not have the

127

same sense of connectedness and cohesion and ended up disbanding and disappointing.

With the emergence of Facebook, the women from the original group all re-connected more fully and someone suggested we re-unite; after all, it had been twenty years since we first sat down in circle together and it was time to celebrate our anniversary! I offered my house as a venue, as I have the most room and am central to everyone and still live in Sacramento.

Tera had been raising two young boys and was excited to leave them at home in Santa Rosa with Dad and get a fix of some female energy! She arrived next. One of our former members had introduced her to her husband years ago. The rest of us divorced while she got married! I remember her wedding day so clearly up on Mt Tamalpais under the trees...she was a picture, tall short blonde hair and elegant in a simple cream dress and a tiara of flowers in her hair.

Judy and Claudia were currently living in the same house and arrived together. Judy has family in Sacramento and like myself, had stayed. In the twenty years interim, she had developed into an accomplished shaman and hypnotherapist. She is also a wonderful chef and used to cook on some of my retreats after Linda left. Now she runs her own groups, taking people to various venues in Northern California to journey to the depths of their soul. Claudia had joined the group later when most of us had moved on, but she and Judy are STILL in the group, along with some other ladies, so the tradition has endured. She was anxious to meet some of the legendary "original groupies!"

Right behind them came Renie. Tall, thin and super fit and strong, she has always been quite the outdoor action girl. She lives in the foothills of the Sierra Nevada and skis, hikes and flies planes. She spends three months each year in Hawaii with just a tent, a car, a desire for adventure and freedom and no agenda other than staying warm. She says having no fixed plan helps her feel alive and open, taking her out of her predictable known, her familiar

128

comfort zone.

The next to arrive were Sara and her daughter, Samantha, having driven up from the Bay area. Samantha, now twenty, had been immersed in our circle energy as a toddler and was anxious to join us as a full, conscious adult. Sara is a hospice nurse and if your Mom were dying, you could not wish for a better person to prepare her for leaving this body. Sara has always been able to feel and read energy and has developed this skill to a high degree, so she can sense what the dying person needs and how to ease them into transition with grace and love. When Sara was married, it was to her lovely big house and garden that Harry would come to offer yoga classes in the summertime in Sacramento. Sara is the most generous person on the planet, full-figured with gorgeous blond locks cascading over her shoulders... she didn't look a day older. In fact, I noticed all of us had aged rather well. No one really looked so different. Or is it that we stop noticing, so well do we know our close friends?

Joni lives just down the road from me, so of course, the person who lives nearest arrives last! Joni is my heroine, now over seventy and the poster child for taking care of your skin. She is still flawless – and without surgery. That may have something to do with the fact that she is an esthetician! She certainly knows what she is doing, and is still pencil slim lovely and dresses like a model. When she turned fifty-five, the women's group at that time created a "croning ceremony" for her. It was a way to celebrate her entering her "wisdom" years with formal ritual. I remember how beautiful that ceremony was and how much I would want that for me at that age. It seemed far away then but was getting awfully close now.

All the women who had had children had raised fine kids and were noticeably fulfilled with their role as Mothers. Now, as in twenty years ago, the partner aspect for some of the ladies had proven to be a little troublesome, but most were settled with a man and content to make the best of it.

"Ladies, we have fresh poached salmon in wine sauce
129

for dinner, with a salad, rice and green beans. Save room for apple crumble and cream for dessert, you all know how our Jules loves her desserts!"

I'm not denying that – especially Linda's divine homemade goodies slathered in fresh cream!

In the summer time, I practically live outside. My house is a small three bedroom suburban bungalow on a quiet street, its major redeeming feature being the lovely, large yard with pool, lawns and patio. Our summer climate is always warm, sometimes hot, but with a pool to jump in and shady fruit trees in the garden, it's a pleasant environment to relax and enjoy the beautiful Sacramento weather. I had set up the outside dining tables with candles and Christmas lights and we grabbed our plates from the kitchen and headed outside.

"Glass of wine anyone? I have red or white."

Actually only three of us drank. Most of the ladies were pretty clean-living and did not tolerate alcohol well. I, on the other hand, have had lots of practice and enjoy a nightly libation. We took our places at the dining table and for a few moments, there was quiet as we concentrated on dinner.

Yum! Linda's food was as divine as ever! I swear she puts some kind of magic ingredient in her food that makes it taste so much better than anyone else's cooking. We all murmured our appreciation as we wolfed down the fresh salmon and crumble.

"Linda you are the best! I am officially kidnapping you – you are to stay here forever and make my taste buds happy!" Joni was adamant and we all agreed!
Linda laughed. "OK well at least I'll be here till Monday! After that you'll have to negotiate with my husband!"

I have to admit, I was terribly excited to see everyone again and see how we had all changed and what we had learned about life and ourselves in the last twenty years. We caught up on practical matters over dinner, talking about our living situations and work and kids, whilst all anticipating the deeper issues to come when we sat down in circle together.

The ladies did not disappoint.

Shaman Judy started us off by calling in the four directions. She invoked the spirits of the north, the east, the south and the west whilst banging her Shaman's drum. The energy in the room quickened and thickened. Everyone took a cushion and we sat down in the middle of the living room floor to tune into each other and the energy present. The moment we came together in circle, that yummy familiar energy returned. I felt like I had come home; embraced by the collective sacred feminine, loved unconditionally, accepted in my totality by these dear friends who knew me so well and had endured all my earlier dramas with so much grace. Being with them made me feel as though I was wrapped in a soft, down comforter of love. I was with my peers. For once, it was not me having to hold the group energy or lead the activities. We all shared in this. I found myself relaxing more and more deeply into our group energy.

We always used a "talking stick" to signify that the person sharing needed our undivided attention. Linda had made the original one and brought it with her. When someone felt the need to speak, they grabbed the talking stick and shared what they were experiencing. One by one, the stick was passed around the circle. The sharing felt deep, true, raw, connecting. The ladies stayed with what was alive for them in the moment, their gratitude to be here together, their pain, their joy. The past, being dead and gone, was not mentioned.

I noticed a sense of groundedness and solidity in the women that had not been present before to the same extent. We had all found our callings in our own way and were living out our purpose. These women were no longer anxious about how their lives would unfold. Their lives HAD unfolded – they were all joyfully carrying out their personal dharma, all helping to raise consciousness in the communities in which they lived.

131

We sat together for a couple of hours as the candles on the mantelpiece burned down. No one wanted to break the energy and leave. But eventually, that old nemesis, the female bladder, called us one by one to the bathroom and the spell was broken. The ladies who had traveled from far away to be here were tired from their journeys and soon settled down for the night.

****

The next day, the weather was warmer and we spent a fair amount of time in the pool cooling down and playing, drying off on blankets under the fruit trees and chatting merrily. There were still some apricots left on the trees and the peaches were starting to ripen too.

"You guys, you've got to help me eat this fruit... please take a big bag and fill it up and take fruit home with you." I passed out some plastic bags and the ladies started to pick the ripe fruit.

It was during one of these relaxed moments that I asked them a question.

"So what age would you rather be? Thirty or fifty?"

It was unanimous – "Fifty" they chorused! "Without a doubt!" added Sara.

I asked them why.

"I don't let things bother me like I used to. I no longer sweat the small stuff," said Renie.

Sara was adamant..."I feel in control of my life and myself. I now have the ability to deal with whatever life throws my way. I feel more powerful and life has more choice-points."

"There are fewer ups and down, more equanimity," Tera, chimed in from behind the apricot tree. I spread a blanket out next to the pool and sat down, anxious to take in every word.

"I understand myself now and know my boundaries and

132

how to ask for what I need and want," added Joni.

"I no longer want my life to be any different from the way it is. I'm grateful for things as they are. Ambitions and expectations are gone and I'm tons happier," said Linda. "Also, I live life more simply now. I know I do not need material possessions to make me happy, just good friends, good healthy food and lots of time in nature."

Renie had jumped in the pool. She raised her head up from the water and shouted, "My relationships are way better, with family, significant others, friends and colleagues. That alone does wonders for my own sense of fulfillment and happiness."

Given my own state of hormonal imbalance and general crankiness, I was frankly a little surprised at how sure they all were about this. Yet they really did seem happier now than twenty years ago. Was I?

Oprah said once that the fifties is the life we are meant to live. I wonder how true this is for the majority of women? Are we improving like fine wines or sliding inexorably towards the grave in a dull haze of routine and pain? My older women friends had certainly found their power and joy and I was in awe of them. I wanted that for myself. I was not feeling very powerful at that time, on the contrary, I felt like I was running on less than all cylinders, small and contracted.

However, on reflection, I could see that some of these statements were true for me too. Small things really don't bother me like they used to. I know my likes and dislikes more clearly and have no trouble in asking for what I want. My relationships with family and friends are strong and real and I have worked hard to resolve any past issues, so now I feel clear, uncorded with anyone.

These things were true, yet something still felt missing.

I lay on the ground on my blanket and looked up at the peach tree, branches still heavy with fruit. Harry's voice jumped into my head. He had said that we are happiest when our learning curve is at its highest. Maybe that was it

- I missed learning! The last few years I had spent so much time teaching that I had forgotten to be the student. I missed that self-discovery, the unearthing of new talents and passions.

That was the clear message that came in that summer Saturday: DON'T STOP LEARNING! The thought alone sent a shiver of excitement through my body. Harry had also said that we are either expanding or contracting. I felt that in my stagnated state, I was contracting and that did not feel good. It was time to do something about all this. My self-directed homework was to embark on a new path of learning and see what captured my interest now!

It also occurred to me that I could benefit from the company of strong women like these around me on a regular basis. I love the effect of all that feminine energy pouring into my aura. In my thirties, I had needed the support of the other ladies to help me through the ending of my marriage. Now I could use that support again in dealing with aging by gathering with other women to share our experiences, our collective wisdom.

Later that night we put on some music and danced in the living room, swaying, gyrating, rubbing up against each other in improvised animal-like contact play, laughing joyfully as we let our bodies express the joy we felt at being together. It was ecstatic for me and I marveled at how something as simple as dance could allow me to feel so good.

I recalled that in the temples of ancient India, the women were encouraged to dance as their path to God. It was recognized that the nature of *Shakti*, the feminine principle, was one of expression and creativity. Whilst *Shiva*, the male principle, would find his bliss in stillness and emptiness, *Shakti's* was in fullness and movement.

We all have both male and female energies within us. For example, in my work I call on the male side of myself in order to be organized with planning, solid in my commitments and to hold a strong space for my groups. But in my personal life, especially in relationship, it behooves me to come back fully into my feminine energy to balance that strong masculine side, and immersing in the *Shakti* energy of other women is a great way to do it. When I allow my feminine side to express and play, it generates more energy, juice and joy for my life. I feel softer, more receptive and open. That energy in turn becomes an attractor to the opposite sex. Men are drawn to that soft feminine energy like bees to a honey pot and it's been my experience that when I am ready to draw in a man into my life, spending quality time with other women in ways such as this is a good way to do it.

As I looked around at these wonderful women adorning my living room, my heart swelled with gratitude. I had needed these ladies to inspire me to dig deep within myself to find my next step, that I may become my own "woman of power." After all, next year I am fifty-five and I want to be ready and worthy for MY croning ceremony!

Chapter 11

Dateline: August 2011
Finding answers

"The doctor will see you now," the pretty, young assistant said, as she led me to the back office. I looked at her feeling a moment of envy. How old was she? Maybe twenty-nine, thirty? She was tall and slim with a wavy shock of thick, auburn hair and clear, young skin. I bet she can still get turned on at the drop of a hat and can eat a box of doughnuts without gaining a pound. I wondered if she had any idea how her body was going to change in about twenty years time. At that age, I certainly hadn't. Enjoy it all while you can, I thought, somewhat cynically.

I was in the waiting room to see Dr Franco, a naturopathic doctor who prescribes bio-identical hormones, and was awaiting my test results. A couple of weeks ago I had taken a saliva test to see what kind of sorry state my hormones were really in. Was I imagining it all or was there really some depletion going on? I was about to find out.

"Hello Julia, do sit down," he said with a friendly smile as he looked intently at the papers on his desk.

"So how are you feeling today?"

"Fat, frazzled and frumpy," I replied. "Gosh, I'm really hoping you can help me shift this funk I'm in. I've never felt so miserable in my entire life. Not to mention the fact that I can't even remember when I last slept a solid eight hours... maybe last year some time..."

"I'm sure we can help you out. This is all very common. So let's have a look at your results here. I see that your progesterone level is very low, that's going to be affecting you, also your estrogens. Your testosterone is a little high - again, that's common in women your age, but the whole picture is one of imbalance so we will need to have you apply a cream to get your hormones back into balance. You'll probably start to feel better quite quickly."

"Really? That's it? Just put some cream on every day and all will be well?"

"Pretty much, yes. Your hot flashes should calm way down and you will start to sleep better. That will help with the other symptoms too. We will order the cream from the compounding pharmacy and they will ship it to you. Put it on every night before you sleep and the progesterone in it will help you relax. After a few months, we will re-test you and see if we need to tweak the formula. You really can be symptom-free quite quickly once we get this right."

Symptom free? I can hardly believe it!

I left the doctor's office feeling hopeful! This would be a modern-day miracle if it works. I could hardly wait to find out. I had discovered that Hollywood stars were also doing this... Suzanne Somers has been writing books about how to age well for years and swears by bio-identical hormones. She looks amazing! And have you seen Jane Fonda recently, now in her seventies? She still looks gorgeous. These women are spearheading the way to healthy aging and redefining what it means to grow old gracefully. Of course, they are superstars with plenty of money and time to spend on keeping themselves lovely, fit and healthy. Still, there is an army of older women out there who are re-inventing what it means to be over fifty in the twenty-first century.

Did you know there are more women alive today over fifty than ever before in recorded history? In fact, two-thirds of all people who have EVER lived to be over sixty-five are alive today! It's funny to think that a hundred or so years ago, very few of us would have even lived this long; so many women died in child-birth or from nutritionally-related diseases. For those who did live into their fifties, they were considered "washed-up" and "on the shelf" by the onset of menopause. They looked older, dressed older and acted older than most of us.

We are a different breed. We have biological and chemical research at our fingertips to help us decide what supplements best support our bodies and what foods nourish our body types the best. There are many women who have the financial means to afford such luxuries, who engage in a healthy lifestyle and who take better care of themselves than women of bygone eras had any way of doing.

Besides, we have teeth. Modern western dental hygiene, regular flossing and fillings have extended the life of our teeth way longer than ever before. Keeping our teeth maintains our face shape and enables us to chew. You only need to go to the third world to see the difference that makes. In Asia I see so many people over forty who are gummy and toothless and stinky with raging gum disease, aged before their time and certainly not what we would call kissable.

I was born when my Grandmother was my age now. As a toddler I remember her teeth sitting in a glass in the bathroom at night. They were a little scary – I had nightmares of them jumping out and biting me. Nana wore sensible shoes and tweed skirts and had absolutely no intention of dating anyone else after her husband died. Her hair was permed and she let it grow gray naturally. She was definitely not what we would call sexy.

It's hard to imagine her only being my age, yet in the early sixties, at least in small-town England, her choices were limited by the society in which she lived. About all that was on offer as far as any fun was a little footsie down at the bridge club and a couple of extra martinis at a Christmas party if you were lucky! The idea of pursuing 'youthfulness and pleasure' would have been a foreign concept, as foreign as celibacy and isolation would be to me. Aging was accepted and tolerated.

As far as I knew, Nana had only been with one man her

whole life, my Grandfather. He died when I was four. Nana was fit, active, bright and as lovely a person to be around as any I know, but she lived the next forty years of her life alone and celibate. I do wonder how Nana felt inside, if her desires were still strong, if she ever felt frisky or got lonely.

I had one clue that maybe she did. The April of my eighth year, my parents already divorced, Dad took Nana and I to Barbados for a two-week vacation. I have clear memories of my first experience of a beautiful Caribbean island, with its swaying palm trees, white-sand beach and steel drum band playing at the hotel restaurant. Nana was really there to baby-sit me so Dad could go out at night, but one day, there was a cocktail party at the Governor's mansion and somehow Dad and Nana both got invited and a local lady came to the room to baby-sit for me.

The next morning, I woke up to find Dad already up but Nana nowhere to be seen.

"Where's Nana? How was your party?" I asked innocently.

"Your Nana disgraced herself last night," said Dad with a grin! "She drank three glasses of Planter's Punch, made a pass at some old geezer and fell down on the lawn spilling her drink all over her dress! I was mortified! We had to take her home early and put her to bed. She's sleeping it off..."

The rest of the day, Nana was quiet and slept a lot. Dad had to get some mileage out of the story and teased her mercilessly about her drinking. I'm sure Nana was highly embarrassed about it all, having transgressed her own social code of conduct and decorum. She always liked to do what was 'proper'.

In the formal, traditional world of Newmarket, England, Nana was "Mrs. Tindall" to her friends, who were called "Mrs. East" and "Mrs. Mills" and would refer to each other in that way. Their connection with each other seemed formal and superficial compared to how I relate to my friends and certainly none of them would ever dream of touching. Other than holding her grandchildren or going to the hairdresser or podiatrist, Nana never got touched. She had never had a massage in her life and would never dream of giving anyone a hug.

Her granddaughter is in a wholly different place. Between then and now, the sexual revolution of the sixties has changed everything. We now live in a world offering far more choices and potential for connection, expansion, youthful aging and pleasure. I have great teeth and will dye my hair blond till the day I die. I hug everyone and enjoy cuddling with friends on the couch, male or female, sharing back rubs or foot massages. Hell, I run around naked at Harbin and enjoy a level of intimacy with my friends that would make my grandmother turn in her grave! My friends and I share how we feel in great detail, which to our generation seems normal and healthy and to hers would have been inappropriate and shocking.

How times have changed, and so rapidly.

In Nana's day, there was no such thing in England as a Health Food Store. Now there is a mountain of life-extension products and recommendations for healthy aging, should we choose to use them. Many of us do. My Mom thinks I'm crazy to eat so many supplements every day, but I believe in Dr Oz and what he and my natural health practitioners say; that we would be insane NOT to take basic daily vitamins, oils and amino acids.

Besides, it seems to be working.

I discovered that before I could get a prescription for bio-identical hormones, I needed a full blood test, which I did in England using our very wonderful National Health Service. When I walked into the doctor's office a day or two after my test, the doctor said ominously,

"Hello Julia. You have very unusual results."

Christ, I thought. What ever is wrong with me?

"You have absolutely nothing wrong with you. Your results are completely within the normal range. And that is NOT normal for a woman your age."

I was so relieved! And particularly happy to hear that as I have only minimal insurance coverage in the USA and cannot afford to be sick.

So here I am... fifty-four, fit, healthy, about to get my hormones balanced and sort my life out. I look around and see so many others like me, a legion of wise women over fifty in young-looking bodies, offered so many choices of how to live and what to do, choices my grand-mother never had in her small-town world.

As consciousness changes we are evolving along with our ability to preserve the physical body, which will give rise to a baby-boom generation of healthy, vibrant older people. We have never had so many older women with money, time, health, wisdom and higher consciousness on the planet. For the first time, women in droves can do what they feel like doing and not what they have to do.

A spiritual teacher I once saw said, "The mature western woman will save the world." So who is this new woman? What is her profile? Are we her?

Paul Ray identified twenty million people in the USA alone that he called 'The Cultural Creatives'; people who think outside the box, who are fueling the demand for things like organic food, clean energy, health supplements and retreat centers. Women over fifty are an important segment of that group and where they choose to put their collective spending power, time and energy will affect the greater population for years to come.

(Ray, Paul H.; Sherry Ruth Anderson (2000). The Cultural Creatives: How 50 Million People Are Changing the World (illustrated ed.). New York: Harmony Books)

Some of the characteristics of these 'cultural creatives' are as follows: they exhibit a love of nature and have a strong awareness of planetary issues such as climate change and poverty, together with a desire to see solutions; they

141

often volunteer for one or more good causes; they place emphasis on maintaining relationships and developing their own unique gifts; they have a strong interest in spiritual and psychological development and want to be involved in creating a new and better way of life.

The Cultural Creative woman has an inquiring mind and makes her own decisions. We could call her a conscious, independent thinker. She makes time for introspection and spiritual study. She may well have taken up yoga or t'ai chi. She is less concerned with the accumulation of material objects and more interested in finding joy in the simple things of life - nature, community, friends, gatherings.

So what's the opportunity here, both for us as individuals and society as a whole? How will we as a group impact our culture, our race, those that follow us? How can we use our remaining time on the planet to share love, spread joy and leave a positive legacy that enriches the world? So many people I know feel purposeless. Maybe just asking these questions could help point women towards new activities that would ignite their fire to continue to live healthy fulfilled lives.

My friend Alice is retired with a good pension and is putting her time and energy into supporting social causes, not just being the change but helping change along. She helps with fund-raising for her pet causes and gives talks. Sandra is devoting her time to animal welfare. Barbara is writing poetry, Jane does her art and my Mom is planting roses, enriching the world with beauty.

Retired people may have thirty or forty years ahead of them to explore life. What is their responsibility here to themselves and to society? What can they become? Is there literally a new species evolving, of conscious, fit older people?

Clearly, not everyone is making life-affirming choices. There is a bifurcation taking place, a fork in the road. There are those who are overweight, unhealthy and inactive by choice, resulting in a very different quality of life. A junkfood-eating, smoking, television-addicted person of

142

sixty can look twenty years older than others of the same age who lead a healthy life-style. They may live till a ripe old age with the help of medications but their energy level may well be too low to contribute much of value as they age.

Which do we choose?

I know which fork I choose. I want to become a "Woman of Power" as I age. I have some work to do to get there from my current state of being, but it's a work in progress and despite the growing pains I am currently experiencing, I am excited for my own transformation. I am encouraged that eventually a stronger 'me' will emerge.

For that to happen some action steps need to be taken…

Chapter 12

Dateline: September 2011
Woman of power

"Hi Joan, I've got us a table here in the corner," I shouted excitedly when I saw my friend's car pull up at the restaurant. She gracefully stepped out of her Volkswagen and walked towards me with a smile.

"It's so good to see you! It's been way too long..."

We gave each other what my Mother calls "California hugs" and I took a good long look at my sweet friend.

"Joan you look terrific! Absolutely radiant! Come on inside and tell me what's been going on."

Joan-Marie is a fellow yoga teacher, artist and massage therapist and is a couple of years older than me. She is a sexy, vibrant, fit woman and I respect her greatly. As part of my "woman of power action steps" I had decided to spend some time with Joan as I see her as an inspiring older woman and wanted to see what could be learned from her.

Many years ago, we had bonded by creating the world's first partner yoga video together. After weeks of rehearsal and shooting, we ended up with a playful, informative product that showcased our talents and love of yoga. We were terribly excited when Yoga Journal picked it as video of the month and went on to sell many copies on our behalf. Since then, we have been good friends, studying yoga together, taking a trip to Greece together one year and enjoying each other's company whenever our schedules allowed.

Joan-Marie has always impressed me as a woman who knows who she is and is comfortable in her own skin. She

144

recently took up pole dancing (she calls it her vertical ballet barre!) and converted her garage into a Goddess temple! (I had a go at the pole and found it to be way harder than it looks!) I had not seen her for way too long so had invited her to lunch at my favorite Thai restaurant to ask her how she was coping with aging. After the food was ordered, we dived right into the topic of my inquiry.

"I'm choosing to see hot flashes as power surges of fiery brilliance," she exclaimed, light shining in her eyes. "Rather than being a victim of internal heat, I like to think of it as a purifying force, burning up past karmas or anger, transforming me into a higher vibration."

Now that was a different way to see it.

"I'm also really exploring the spiritual side of my sexuality, both through ritual and meditation. My body is changing, but I see it as an invitation to open to other more potent parts of myself that I had ignored as a younger girl."

"Sounds like you are creating your own authentic tantra practice," I said, with enthusiasm, as the waitress delivered two steaming helpings of *pad thai*. "Besides, that's something you can enjoy on your own, no partner needed."

"Exactly," agreed Joan. "I'm single right now but can still make sweet love to myself, offering the fruit of my devotion to the Divine. It feels wonderful."

Joan is inspiring. Just being around her makes me feel more alive, more hopeful and expanded.

She continued as we ate.

"I have stopped making vaginal decisions! Now that I am no longer ruled by my biology I am making wiser choices around men. I feel I am not as manipulating or as easily manipulated. It's a more relaxing and peaceful way to live.

"Also I challenge all women over fifty-five to redefine what "crone" means to them. For global change to occur, it may be up to us, the mature western woman, to awaken and empower ourselves as individuals and use our influence to be the change we want to see."

Yes! I want to be part of that change! Joan is right – we as a group have immense power and potential.

" I agree. There are internet movements going around right now that encourage us to put our money in credit unions and not continue supporting the big banks; and to support local farmers rather than big business supermarkets."

"Right. There are so many simple changes we can make with our consumer spending power that collectively make a huge difference."

"You know Joan, I am thinking of starting a woman's group. Are you interested in getting involved?"

Last week I had put out a call via my email list to see who was interested in a new woman's group. The response was overwhelming... about twenty-five women responded, saying they would love to be part of a power circle.

"Absolutely! There is such a need for women to support each other. Let me know if you'd like me to come and offer a meditation or something."

I am lucky to have a friend like her. We finished a delightful lunch and vowed to get together more regularly. Really, the men in our lives may come and go but our true women friends are there for the duration. Nurturing my female relationships is one of the most important ways I can spend my time.

Not all my friends are doing so well. After many years of serving a family, some women have lost the ability to even know what makes THEM happy. Take my friend Gwen, for example.

Gwen is at a choice point. After thirty years of marriage and with the kids grown up and gone, she finds herself left with a distant, workaholic husband. She is starting to question the sanctity of her marriage vows and ask what it is she really wants from life. Who is she now that she is no longer a Mother? She recognizes that she has had a habit of

146

giving her power away to kids and husband, letting their needs be met before her own. Now she must learn to stand up for herself all over again. It's not her habit. She usually just goes along with everyone else's wants.

But is it still appropriate for her to be playing the role of meek, mild housewife? Or can she become a woman of power? What will she choose? Comfort, safety and familiarity, pleasing kids and husband at her expense, even thought her kids are now adults? Or taking the risk to speak up for what she wants in her life now, even though that may not go down well with her family?

A woman of power has enough awareness to make good choices for herself. She would rather be alone than compromise her values. In my experience, personal autonomy is a pre-requisite to becoming a woman of power, be that as a single person or within a partnership.

At least I have that one right. I have chosen to live alone for the past ten years, enjoying the autonomy of owning my own house and having the right to ask a man to leave if the relationship was not working. My freedom is precious and affords me the luxury of being choosy with whom I spend my time. My house is my cave. I get to retreat to it and can choose to spend time alone or invite friends to be with me as I please.

Meanwhile, I had taken to heart the notion of needing to learn something new and had decided to try a dance class. Last Wednesday I'd gone to the local dance studio for a salsa lesson.

****

The studio was hopping as I shyly pushed the main door open, crowded with dancers, salsa music blaring from the stereo. On the brightly lit dance floor directly in front of me, couples were twirling expertly around the room, feet moving impossibly fast, movements magically synchronized together.

Oh my, I would LOVE to   be able to dance like that!

147

I wondered how many years of practice it took to be that accomplished.

"Welcome to Zara's studio," said the petite brunette at the front desk with a smile. "Which class are you here for? We have foxtrot starting in ten minutes or beginners salsa."

"I'm here for the salsa," I said. "And these people dancing over there, how long have they been at this?"

"That's the intermediate class, so about three to six months."

That's all? Could I do that if I practiced?

The thought was certainly appealing, but as I have never had much affinity and grace for dance of any kind, it seemed like a faraway prospect.

As the dancers cleared the floor, a trim young girl of about twenty-five came out and changed the music in the CD player. She put something much slower on, still Latin-style, but with a beat mere mortals could move to, and asked everyone to line up behind her. There were about twelve ladies and fourteen men in the class, most of them looking about as awkward as I felt. Still, I was here and going to give this a shot.

"Hello everyone, I'm Dawn. I'm going to teach you the basic steps of salsa. It's a simple one two three pattern. Step right, follow with the left foot, step in place with the right foot, like this." She demonstrated the steps. We followed her.

OK that was pretty easy. I can do that.

It looked not even remotely similar to what the dancers I saw earlier were doing, but I guess we all start somewhere.

"One, two, three. One, two, three", she counted.

Yes I can do this.

"Now ladies pick a partner and we'll do it together as couples."

I found a tall guy with a pale but sweet face who looked friendly and asked if I could   be his partner.

148

"Sure. This is my first time though. I may not be any good," he muttered quietly.

He turned out to be right. For some reason, he could not move to rhythm! When Dawn shouted 'one', he would move a half second later, so it was terribly hard to follow him, as ladies are supposed to do. We "danced" for a few minutes then Dawn yelled, "Switch! Ladies move a partner to the right!"

An older Mexican-looking man with garlic breath and a droopy mustache was my next partner. He turned out to be surprisingly good! Maybe he grew up dancing to these rhythms. Maybe he he was a natural-born dancer. Either way, I noticed he held me with confidence and moved easily to the beat. I could relax, knowing he had me, which allowed me to move my hips with more swagger and sway. He actually made me feel like I could dance!

"OK everyone line up again. I'm going to teach you the left-hand turn," said Dawn.

Dawn showed us how to change the basic pattern to move around our partners with the men lifting our hand and we ladies stepping elegantly around them in a twirl. This was more like it! A little salsa rock and roll! We practiced the left side and the right side.

Moving slowly, I could get the steps, but when we paired up as couples again and had to move with the music, my feet somehow lost their memory and I found myself stumbling awkwardly around my man, sometimes losing footing or moving the wrong direction.

"Men, lead your women! A subtle wrist movement will cue the ladies as to the direction you want them to take so they don't have to guess. Now switch partners and try again."

This time I partnered with a short, older, Latino-looking man. He looked Peruvian to me, or maybe Cuban.

Ah, Cuba.

Years ago as a British citizen I had gone to Havana and

149

visited the local dance clubs. The Cubans may well have the plainest cuisine on the planet due to chronic food shortages, but they sure as hell make the best *mojitos* and know how to party! My group found an open-air dance club in the old town that had an all-women salsa band playing. They were brilliant! Such high energy, foot-tapping sounds.

As we sat there watching, a local man came up to me asked me to dance. In my mediocre Spanish, I told him I did not know how.

"Ven conmigo, chicita," he insisted as he took my hand and led me to the dance floor. For the next fifteen minutes, I proceeded to transform into the world's most brilliant British salsa dancer, simply by being expertly guided by this lovely young man! He led me so well with his hands that it was easy to follow him, even without knowing any steps at all. It was exhilarating, surprising and ultimately exhausting. I eventually collapsed in a tired heap back onto my chair and quickly gulped down my patiently waiting *mojito.*

That memory had been the prompt for learning salsa properly... I wanted to learn how to dance this exciting dance and be able to travel to Latin countries and join the locals in their fun and games. Here I am off to Ecuador in a few months, after all. I'd better pay attention.

Back in my Sacramento dance class, Mr. Havana told me his name was Juan and I placed my arm on his shoulder. Sure enough, this man had rhythm. He guided me into turns in a way that I could follow and soon I began to feel more elegant and less clumsy. This was starting to be fun! We whirled and twirled for a few more minutes until our teacher said, "That's all for today, folks. Come back next week for more. See you then."

I left the studio that evening with that same feeling of exhilaration and fullness that I had had in Cuba. I would need to come to a lot of lessons to have any sense of accomplishment in this new activity, but I enjoyed it and would do so. I realized I felt happy and empowered. Yes, Harry was right. Learning IS both fun and necessary.

****

The great news is… the bio-identical hormones are working! My hot flashes are almost gone and I am sleeping so much better. I now wake up in the morning full of energy and feeling motivated and happy again and my mind has regained its sharpness. What a difference! On a physical level, my weight has dropped back down and my metabolism appears to be kicking back up. Plus, when I work out at my Health Club, I notice a sharp increase in my ability to life weights. I am getting stronger and I feel an aliveness that has been absent since that memorable fiftieth birthday party. Could it be that my newfound friend in the form of a hormone cream is really turning back the clock? Could it even be possible that my female mojo has returned, allowing me to embrace normality once again?

I will need my strength. My friend, Janice, has agreed to come to Galapagos with me and we are shooting for the whole month of February 2012. We are both super excited and for me this is a bucket list dream that only a few short months earlier, seemed as impossible as my becoming the Queen of England.

Plus I am working my tail off preparing for my annual jaunt to Asia which includes the insane task of booking thirty-seven individual flights for myself and my students, organizing the best elephant rides known to man in Thailand and sourcing the most beautiful dive sites in the Philippines. Adding to it all I will be visiting Myanmar with my best friend, Sally, for a few days vacation and finishing the trip teaching a tantra workshop in Hong Kong. A magnificent seven weeks of great adventure and unexpected challenge awaits. Let's hope all goes according to plan!

Ten Keys to becoming a Woman of Power

It has occurred to me that I need to draw up my own charter, my own list of reminders that will help me get through this change in my life. My very own... but please adapt it for yourself.

1. Take responsibility for my body. Balance hormones naturally, take appropriate supplements; diet and exercise. A balanced body is the source of my health, radiance and energy for life. It's my responsibility to discover how to bring my body into balance and is a constant exploration. It is sad and shocking to me when I look around and see how many women are ignorant about how to best take care of themselves. In this age, when there are so many great health books and natural doctors abounding, there is no more excuse. We even have TV programs like "The Biggest Loser" and "Dr Oz" to educate and encourage us. There are yoga studios on every street corner and health food stores and naturopathic doctors in most towns.

2. Write my bucket list. I love having a bucket list and am constantly crossing off the experiences I have already had and adding more. It keeps me focused on life goals and excited about my life and my potential. I also believe strongly that writing down our goals helps the Divine to know what we want and aids in attracting those experiences to us.

3. Keep learning. When I continue to repeat my same skill sets and experiences time and again, I become dull and stagnant. The mind loves stimulation and giving it new things to learn helps me to feel alive and happy. Learning about new people, places and things is stimulating and sparks my desire to be the best I can be.

4. Spend time with powerful women or join a woman's group. When I am with powerful women friends, I feel supported, loved and cared for. I learn so much from

152

them. Their wisdom rubs off on me and helps me deal with life's challenges. Immersing in feminine energy is helpful, too, for attracting a strong, masculine man.

5. Leave a positive legacy. As I move into the second half of life, the idea of mortality becomes more real. What can I leave behind me when I am gone? Will the world be a better place because I was here for a few years? Thinking about my legacy helps me focus on the influence I have on others, especially the younger people in my circle. It encourages me to mentor those that have interest in the particular knowledge that I possess. It also challenges me to rise to my potential professionally in the time I have left, completing projects that I may otherwise have put off and initiating new ones that will help to create that legacy.

6. Be in integrity. My word is my power. If I am not truthful, either because I am telling outright lies or manipulating in some way, I am out of integrity and do not deserve to sleep well at night. During my yogic studies with Harry, I discovered the power of being my word and the peace that it brings. This key has held me in good stead most of my adult life and still does today. As part of this key, I must know myself well enough to be able to be authentic and honest and have the courage to express that personal truth.

7. Ask for what I want. This may sound obvious, but so often I have subjugated what I really want to the desires of a man. No more. My next man must honor my wishes and to do so, I have a responsibility to him both to know what they are and to express them clearly.

8. Clean up my past, do my forgiveness work, make amends. If I am still holding on to my past because I have been too lazy to clean up old relationships of every kind, I am losing power and energy. It literally leaks out. As part of this key, I need to come to a place of peace with my relationship with my parents and close family in particular. If it is guilt I am carrying, amends need to be made. I like to scan my past from time to time and ask, "Whom am I still holding energy with?" My goal is to be as free as possible from emotional   baggage.

9. Financial autonomy. I choose to live debt-free, even if it means living simply. When I was swimming in debt and had little or no control over my finances, I felt disempowered and weak, not a good feeling. I also choose financial independence, meaning that even if I should live with a man and we share expenses, I have control of my own money. Every woman deserves at least a portion of disposable income that she can spend any way she chooses.

10. Love. A woman of power is a woman who loves. First and foremost, I must love and accept myself, wrinkles and all. From that sound basis, my love overflows out to all who surround me. It is the main source of all my power, the motivation behind all the other keys. Love is a way of being, our natural state when all else is stripped away. Practicing jnana yoga inquiry and releasing all that no longer serves has helped me to drop more and more deeply into this state of love that defines my life.

(For more detailed help on how to work these keys, please refer to my other two books, "20 Questions for Enlightened Living" and "Your Presence is Enough.")

PART 3

ASIA

Chapter 13

Dateline October 10th, 2011
Bali

I LOVE BALI! Although the South area has been very developed and continues to get more congested with each passing year, I still find it to be the most sacred of isles, where the people hold strong devotional heart energy. I take a yoga group to Bali every October. In fact, I've been doing that for twelve years now, way before anyone had read "Eat, Pray, Love." But I will admit that when I read the book, I was curious about both the medicine man, Ketut Liyer, who had predicted author Elizabeth Gilbert's future with astonishing accuracy, and the healer, Wayan, who had helped Elizabeth with a health issue.

Two years ago, three of my friends, Stella, Judith and Joni, were part of my yoga group in Bali and wanted to join me on a trip to visit him. Joni, a long-time friend from my woman's group, just turned seventy and looking fabulous; Judith, an avid dancer and Bay area native; and Stella, a lanky head-turner of a blond in her early thirties and in Asia for the first time. I don't know who was more curious about whom, the locals who could not stop staring at her, or Stella, gaping at all she saw in this so foreign a landscape.

On our first night in Sanur, Stella and Judith had persuaded me to go dancing with them at a local nightclub. It was fun, but I have to admit that despite great music, my fifty-year old bones screamed for my bed around 11.00pm whilst the young'uns danced till the wee hours – a reminder that my priorities were different now. No longer interested in cute Aussie guys, I was just as happy to retreat to the comfort of my hotel room and a great novel after an hour or so of boogying down.

We had since left the coast and were staying at Alam

Indah Hotel near Ubud, my favorite hotel in the whole world. It turned out that Ketut's family compound was only five minutes away from Nyuh Kuhning, the village where the hotel is located.

One morning, after breakfast, we excitedly piled into the hotel van and asked our driver to take us to see Ketut. After a short drive, our van dropped us off outside his family compound, next to the sign declaring, "Ketut Liyer, Healer." Every traditional doorway in Bali is ornate with carving and this one was no exception. Exquisite stone images of Barong, the protector God, were carved with precision into the stone above the doorway along with decorative flowers and animal figures. The door itself was heavy and wooden, with a large brass handle and yet more carving decorating its panels. With some intrepidation, myself and the three other ladies stepped inside.

It was quiet inside the compound, a contrast from the busy street noise outside. A Balinese family generally lives together in a community, with separate sleeping areas for individuals, a communal kitchen, bathroom, meeting area and family temple. It's all clustered around a central courtyard with chickens clucking, dogs roaming and even the odd family duck pecking for grubs.

Ketut's son greeted us. It was clear he was an educated person, well-dressed like a businessman and speaking perfect English. He invited us to sit down in the waiting area as Ketut was currently with someone else. That was fine with us. It gave us a chance to look around a bit and absorb the peaceful atmosphere. We saw some paintings on the wall. This was Ketut's artwork, lovely drawings of Gods and Demons, a favorite theme for Balinese artists, plus some nature scenes. Ubud is known for its artists and craftsmen and it was clear that Ketut inherited that same artistic gene.

After about twenty minutes, the son returned and told us Ketut was ready to see us. Ketut was sitting on his porch, just like in the book and the same one used for the movie. There was a picture of Elizabeth Gilbert above his head. And yes, he did look very old, with one prominent tooth

157

protruding down from otherwise vacant gums. He was welcoming and curious about us, too, wanting to know where we were from and where we were staying. Then one by one, he gave us a palm reading.

He told us all we were going to live to be over one hundred and that we would find another man to marry (we were all single at the time). He looked at our backs and touched in a couple of places, offering a little advice on staying young and healthy.

At one point he said to me, "You can be make love three times a night, but not more."

Three times a day, every day?

I was impressed with his confidence in my lovemaking appetites. Maybe in another life when I had infinite time and energy for such things.... or maybe it was something to aspire to in this one. Now there's a concept. What would it take for me to want to make love three times a day every day? Food for dreams, no doubt. However, when he got to Stella he declared with a glint in his eye that she could make love as many times a night as she wanted! How she smiled!

It was all absolutely charming. I don't think he stopped grinning once and although he kept apologizing that his English was bad, it was actually quite decent, just heavily accented. We left very happy to have met him, still in the dark as to his healing powers or real medicine man wisdom, but pleased nonetheless to have connected with so lovely a man. As we left, a local couple walked in to see him with a chicken as an offering. Plain out of chickens that day, we had left him cold, hard cash instead.

Last year, I wanted to take my group to see him again, but that darn Julia Roberts was there filming the 'Eat, Pray, Love' movie, so we could not go. Curiously, the actor who played Ketut in the movie looked just like him, except he was missing that one, dangling front tooth.

This year I am back in Ubud with a lovely group of ten students. Amongst them is Deborah, one of my dearest

158

friends, who is celebrating her sixtieth birthday here this week. When I asked her what she wanted from the group for her gift, she was very clear.

"I want to go and see Wayan, the Balinese herbalist that Elizabeth Gilbert befriended," she said excitedly. "That's been top of my bucket list ever since I read about her. Do you think there's any way to make that happen?"

"I'll do my best," I replied, hoping the waiting time to see so famous a lady would not stretch into weeks.

The next day, while the rest of the group were out hiking in the paddy fields with our lovely Balinese guide, Darta, I took the van to visit Wayan's office to see what I could do for Deborah.

Her office was in a quiet street and a little tucked away. Our driver had some difficulty even finding it. Like most places in Bali, it was open to just walk in. I saw who I presumed was Wayan upstairs, massaging a Western lady. Another lady was sitting at a small table, apparently waiting, so we chatted.

"This is Wayan's healing center, right?" I asked for confirmation.

"Yes, she's right up there working on my sister." The lady had an Australian accent.

"Is this the first time you've been here?"

"No, we came last year and really liked her treatment. She scans you and gives you herbs and a diet plan, plus some teas to take at home. The teas were really strong and put us both into detox and we threw up for two days solid, but after that, we both felt tons better."

I looked around the center. There were jars and jars of herbs lining the cupboards and old, yellowing charts of the body and skeleton on the walls. A small kitchen was next to the entranceway where all manner of vegetables were sitting out on the counter, ready to be made into a healthy lunch.

After a few minutes, the Australian lady upstairs

159

emerged looking flushed but happy. Wayan followed her down the stairs, acknowledging me with a nod, but staying focused on completing her instructions to her client on the protocol that would be best for her. She is a thickset, strong looking lady of around forty with a commanding presence and limited English. Wearing the traditional sarong and silk top of the Balinese, Wayan had wavy, dark hair and an easy smile.

When she was done with the Australian ladies, I introduced myself and arranged an appointment for Deborah for the next day. How excited she would be! I could hardly wait to see her delight when I gave her the news!

****

"Oh you did it! This is the best birthday ever!" exclaimed Deborah when I told her we were going to see Wayan at 11:00 a.m. the next day, which actually WAS her birthday! "I can't wait to meet her and see what she says!"

"I've booked you a body scan and future reading," I told her, happily. "I'll come with you and take notes so you can just relax and absorb it all."

The next day we landed once more at Wayan's hidden little healing center and found her waiting for us.

"Come in Deborah and fill out form."

She ushered us inside to the little table and pointed to a photocopied form that had us trying hard not to laugh when we read it! It asked the most compelling but cutely worded questions:

Brain line.... little smart, big smart or brilliant?

Married... deep love, or not too deep love?

Spiritual... are you more lazy, or diligent?

Love... people might have fallen in love with you but you did not, or you may have fallen in love but they did not?

160

Sexuality... strong sex, or if older, sex more lowly?

Generations... how many generations reincarnation you come from?

Deborah sat down and filled out the form as best she could. Although she had absolutely no idea how many generations of reincarnation she came from.

While Deborah was filling out the form, Wayan smudged herself with a herbal smoke stick and did her prayers, asking the Gods for permission to read and heal the body. That granted, she examined the form then asked Deborah to stand up.

The first thing she did was to take her hands and feel their energy. She looked at her nails, touched her belly and started to speak.

"Too much sugar. Too acid. Not enough calcium. Need more vitamin E. You lazy with taking care of body. You need to get back in balance"

Wayan was a straight shooter. She spoke it as she saw it, no editing for Western sensibilities.

Then she looked at her palm to see what the lines revealed.

"You have two big heartbreaks in your life. You live long time. You have one man love you but you don't love him.

I took notes allowing Deborah to fully absorb the experience.

"You go to bathroom now and put on sarong. You need me massage. And detox."

Once she had changed into her sarong, a little Balinese man materialized as if out of nowhere and rubbed her down vigorously with special leaves that have exfoliating and detoxifying properties. Deborah emerged ten minutes later with a glow on her face and body.

"I'm already feeling fantastic! Those leaves sure perked my energy right up!"

161

Wayan had already gone upstairs.

"Come on up here and lie on table."

She proceeded to massage Deborah in a directed but firm way that reminded me of our Maori healer friends from New Zealand. Not a relaxing spa massage this, but a specific treatment to get energy moving where it had been stagnant. Wayan poked a stick under Deborah's arm to stimulate lymph, which elicited a sharp yelp from the recipient!

"Ow! That hurts!"

"You feel better after," assured Wayan, taking a bottle of hot oil and rubbing her belly.

After about forty minutes, Deborah emerged a new woman! Glowing, relaxed and super clean, she left with some of Wayan's special herbal teas, lots of great advice and a huge smile on her face! The experience had felt very authentic and I could see why Elizabeth Gilbert had been so attracted to this wonderful woman. Wayan is a true woman of power, working her purpose with her own business and helping people in an authentic way. It was also a good reminder to me that I needed to be "not lazy" and keep my own health in good balance. Maybe then I would not need a sharp stick up my armpit!

****

After Ubud, I take my group through the central mountains, passing coffee fields, lake temples and vineyards, heading west until we almost reach Java. We end our trip at a lovely, quiet hotel called Taman Sari at Pemuteran beach in the northwest of the island where few tourists go. The hotel is next to an ancient fishing village and a couple of beautiful old temples.

Many years ago, Agung Prana, now the owner of the hotel, came to see some relatives in the village. He went down to the beach at sunset and heard the voice of God:

"Build a hotel."

The message was clear.

"But this is just a messy, local fishing village that no tourists ever visit. Why ever would I want to build a hotel here?" thought Agung. At that time the beach was strewn with trash and the coral reef had been pretty much destroyed by local fishing methods that dynamited the reef to collect the dead fish.

"*Build a hotel.*" The voice in his head came in loud and clear again.

Agung had always been a spiritual man and he knew the voice of God when he heard it. So he started to think about the possibility. He already had a hotel in the south of Bali and was a well-to-do businessman. He definitely had the funding to make it happen. But this part of Bali was very rural, with an uneducated population, subsistence farming and the kind of simple village life that had remained unchanged for thousands of years. The people were poor and jobs were few. They could certainly use the opportunities hotel employment would bring.

So Agung called a village meeting. He explained to the people how he could make a deal with them. If they would agree to stop destroying their reef, he would agree to fund a hotel that could potentially change their lives for ever, elevating them out of their traditional farming, which was a little dodgy even in a good year. He would train workers and teach them English. Maybe in time some would be groomed for management. He would build schools and introduce medical care, which was pretty much non-existent at that time.

The village chief asked, "Why would the tourists want to come here, to our beach? What would we have to offer them?"

In a stroke of genius, Agung replied, " We will rebuild the reef using the latest technology. The corals will grow again and the fish will return. We will clean the beach and offer dive trips to nearby Menjangan Island." (Menjangan was already a marine reserve with fabulous snorkeling).

163

The chief pondered for a moment – looked at the expectant faces of his people, then said, "OK. I agree. Build your hotel and we will work for you."

This was back in 1997.

In 2000, Agung's little hotel where the mountains reach the sea won an international award for eco-tourism. His brilliant plan to stimulate reef growth through A/C electrical currents connected to rebar twisted in all manner of interesting shapes had born fruit. The reef was growing, the fish were back and people from all over the world were discovering this little piece of paradise, including me. I had stumbled upon the hotel back in 2001 and just loved it. Every year since I had brought my Bali group to Taman Sari for a few blissful days on the beach, snorkeling and diving, or simply kicking back under the sea-grape trees.

Agung and I had become friends and he had even built a yoga pavilion and a meditation room so groups like mine would have a place to practice. He particularly likes to have spiritually inclined groups at the hotel, as the peace and quiet there is conducive for introspection and these groups help to raise the vibration of the area.

Here I was again.

On our last full day at the beach, I found myself sitting under the shade tree after breakfast with three of the older ladies in my group. By that I mean over sixty, so older than me. I had them all pegged as women of power and had some questions for them.

"So we all know the pitfalls of growing older as women, but what is the silver lining?" I asked the three other ladies. "I'm interested to know what your experience has been."

"I can do and say exactly as I please," said Janet, an "Energizer-bunny" lady with not an ounce of fat on her who could run and hike me into the ground and was pushing seventy. "I take the position nowadays that it's perfectly fine to ask for what I want and that I deserve to get my needs met. When I was younger I was way too timid to do that – I would never have dared speak up for

164

what I needed. That feeling of "couldn't care less what people think" gives me a certain power. I feel authentic, whole. I have given up pretending to be different from the way I really am. There's such a freedom in that – it's like I fully accept myself and my humanness and am totally OK with it. I no longer need to be noticed, to be the star. I can sit back and enjoy everything around me without needing to prove myself"

Barbara chimed in: "I love it that I no longer have periods. They were such a pain – literally. Now I no longer have to fear getting pregnant so I feel freer in my lovemaking. In fact sex has gotten better since menopause ended and my hormones balanced out."

Janet continued the thread. "Now that my body no longer needs to reproduce, energy is freed up to be more creative. I have discovered passions I didn't know I had. I am traveling more, getting involved with the environmental movement and hiking groups. I lead such a full life, even though I am single and living alone. Also I get to follow my inner impulses to either be quiet and sit back, or to be more active and serve others and play bigger. But the thing is, I now get to choose which I do."

Anna was with us too. An energy healer from the Bay area, she is tall, blonde and graceful, but has recently had some health challenges. "I am way more compassionate now that I have my own physical issues; and more humble. When I was young, I just could not relate to elderly peoples' aches and pains. Now I have them! I have to accept I will now need to do things differently, with more care."

"That's great to hear," I said, "But I am curious – did any of you have any idea what this menopause transition was going to be like? I mean did your Mother ever sit you down and give you a heads-up like when you were twelve years old and about to start becoming hormonal, or were you part of a woman's wisdom group that clued you in? Because I sure as hell wasn't and I'm wondering what can be done to change that for those that come after us."

At this last comment, everyone became very animated and they all talked at once...

"My Mother was dead before the change happened to her. If you think about it, only a few decades ago, not many women lived to experience menopause so it was rarely discussed in polite society."

"Mine wouldn't have dreamed of discussing such a personal thing!"

"Mine neither."

"Exactly! There needs to be groups of women who help prepare us for this!" said Anna. "I thought I was losing my marbles! The emotional ups and downs were so crazy. I would burst into tears at the slightest thing and sink into deep depressions so easily. It's been really stressful. I went through a tremendous amount of anxiety and fear. I have never been a fearful person, but all of a sudden, small things scared me and I felt smaller in the world, less energetic, contracted."

"No-one tells us what's going to happen when our periods end, only when they begin." said Barbara.

"I had this crazy idea that menopause would never happen to me."

Janet butted in: "Where is the guidance, the support? It certainly doesn't come from the men in our lives unless we are really lucky... they get confused and scared too. In fact my husband took it all personally – my loss of libido was a reflection to him of his own fading prowess and he didn't like it one bit."

"We need training groups for men and women!" I commented. "But what would we call them? Crone groups sounds bloody awful – like we are a bunch of old hags cackling away."

"How about Woman's wisdom groups? And Yoda groups for men?" suggested Anna.

We all liked that idea.

Anna piped up again. "I really would like to have heard other women talk about how it was for them so I could understand it's not just happening to me. I was shocked at the bodily changes – the dry vagina, painful intercourse and the "not feeling good enough" that goes with all that. I have had such a fear of non-lubrication that it's got to the point I just don't want to attempt sex. I feel like a dried up old prune – and that's not sexy. And with that, a whole piece of my past persona has fallen away."

"Yes men really need to be educated that for the older woman it's really important to use lots of lubrication for intercourse. More is better than less," suggested Barbara.

"Hear hear!" we all agreed there.

"Also we need to enlighten men into letting go of the requirement that we ladies have an orgasm! So many men feel that we are "less than" if we don't come, but as we get older, it can harder and harder to reach a climax."

"Yes," I added. "Men are attached to our climax because they think it reflects their abilities. And sometimes it's nothing to do with them – it's just us! That's where tantra practice comes in... if we can all learn that it's about the sacred journey, the wonder of sharing energy and connection rather than going for the goal post all the time. I mean let's face it, all relationships have their phases. Mostly that hot, passionate sexual energy shifts at some point anyway and that is the invitation to work with the tantric energies."

"So how did the men in your lives deal with the changes that were happening for you?" I asked, fanning myself in the heat. Menopausal ladies take note – always carry your hand-fan to the tropics! You will need it!

"My menopause literally happened overnight. I could feel the shift going on in my body and when I told my husband he rolled his eyes and said 'Oh God'," said Barbara.

"I felt less desirable as a woman," admitted Anna, "and very vulnerable. In that emotionally fragile state, I really needed to be held and told I was still OK, still lovable. I needed my man to hold space for the contractions and expansions I was going through and not take it personally. But all my boyfriend cared about was whether he was still going to get laid as much as usual. He had an addiction to porn and when my libido dropped, he turned to that as a way to get his kicks even more so. I felt so rejected. Needless to say, that relationship didn't last."

Janet's face suddenly brightened. "My girlfriend's husband was marvelously supportive. When she entered menopause, he asked if she would like to take a year off from him and her life just to be with herself and adjust to this new reality. He said she had been Mother and wife and now it was time for her to follow her dreams. She would just need time to figure out what they were."

"Now that's what I call love!" I chimed.
"Yes. It's great when our past history has created enough of a binding agent to allow our men to stand by us and support us through this."

"How do you feel when your man stares at younger women?" I inquired.

"Left out, insignificant, envious, small, not good enough, inadequate, angry..." I heard the comments.

Anna continued, "But on the other side, I find now that when a cute guy walks in the room I think, *oh pretty,* but I don't have that desire to chase after him like I used to. My boyfriends tongue still hangs out over young cute chicks though in some Pavlovian fashion. It's a different response."

"How we are when we are sixty begins at thirty," said Barbara, a fabulously gorgeous and empowered woman in her early sixties.

I thought this was profound. A steady diet of yoga, disciplined exercise and good eating habits begun at an early age surely bear fruit as we age. Barbara was proof of that pudding. She looked great and was strong from regular workouts, flexible from daily yoga, more than many twenty-somethings. As a yoga teacher, I see this in my students. Many young people raised on a diet of fast food and without regular exercise are in far worse shape then someone with a trained body like Barbara. Her biological age is probably closer to theirs and her organs in better shape.

We were all quiet for a moment and our shared words hung thick in the air like a winter fog. I was aware of a bird chirping its unique song in the tree overhead and felt the gentle, warm breeze on my skin.

Then Janet broke the silence. "I feel like I need to grieve my loss of youth, fertility and sexiness. I know I need to honor the choice that I made to not have children, but I still need to grieve the barren womb."

"And I need to grieve the two abortions I had. I can never have more babies now."

This hit home as true and necessary to me. "For sure – without acknowledging that the fertile part of our life is now over, we cannot move on cleanly to the next stage of our lives."

Anna was thinking our loud..."Sounds like this need for grieving is crying out for a ritual of some kind."

"Yes, we should create one," added Barbara. "Let's get together when we get home and do a grief ritual for our fertility!"

I looked at my friends with amazement. This conversation had made them come alive in a way I had not seen before. They were animated and engaged, leaning towards each other almost in a huddle, as though to keep our sharing secret. Their eyes were shining, and the energy around us was palpable.

"This feels like a really important conversation and I would love to continue it, but I have a massage appointment in a few minutes," said Barbara, who incidentally is a therapist.

"See you later," we chorused, as everyone started to

move and go about their day.

What would it be like to talk about these ideas with more women? What else could be shared? What new ways of helping others transition into menopause could be concocted?

It certainly gave me lots of ideas to run by my new woman's group once I got home. I pondered the thought as I took some quiet time for myself and rested under the sea grape trees, occasionally popping into the water to cool down and check out the fish activity around the reef.

****

Later that same day, the hotel manageress cornered me and said, " Julia, you really should take your group down to the temple tonight. It's October full moon and just once a year the Pondok Sari temple on the seafront comes alive with people doing ceremonies. It's a very sacred, special day to us and you may enjoy participating."

Yes!

I alerted the group and at 5:40 p.m. we squeezed into a minivan for the fifteen-minute journey along the coast to the temple.

There was full pandemonium as we arrived. Normally serene and quiet, this temple by the sea had been descended upon by a seething mass of people, all anxious to bear their offerings of fruit, cookies and rice and receive blessings from the temple priests.

We walked with many locals up the ancient stone steps and entered the temple grounds, taking sunset pictures over the ocean through the beautiful stone-carved walls. We were the only foreigners, yet the locals didn't seem to mind and gawked at us as much as we admired them - their beauty, their elegant costumes of lace tops and sarongs for the women and special temple day hats and sarongs and smart shirts for the men. All looked cool and comfortable while we sweated in the humidity.

170

Inside the grounds there was an inner area where hundreds of Balinese were sitting, awaiting their turn for a blessing. We looked on from the outside, wondering if it was OK to take pictures. As I was watching, a lovely lady walked up to me and in perfect English asked if we would like to join her and her family for prayers!

Would we ever!

With much gratitude, we followed her and her drop-dead gorgeous twenty year-old daughter, Didi, into the inner temple area. They graciously gave us flowers to pray with and invited us to sit with them. It turned out they had driven sixty kilometers to be here, as this special ceremony only happens once a year and is important to their family.

Everyone was chattering and excited; very different from our church atmosphere. In a nod to our modern world, Didi was tweeting to her friends on her Blackberry like any other young person. Suddenly the gamelan orchestra started playing loudly and a priest chanted over the loud speaker.

"Om, shanti, shanti..."

We followed suit as the family bowed their heads and placed their hands together. Time to pray.

I was just starting to say my gratitudes to God for this wonderful journey and auspicious moment when suddenly it was all over! Maybe I am long-winded, but it seemed awfully quick to me, maybe two minutes or so!

After that, the priest, all dressed in white for purity, came to each person in turn and sprinkled holy water on them with some kind of stick that he dipped into a bowl. First the water was sprinkled on the head, then three times onto the open hands, to be licked, then once more on the head. Finally some white rice was applied to the third eye point and the blessing was complete.

The whole process took about twenty-five minutes.

The gamelan orchestra started up again with much enthusiasm as people filed out of the inner sanctuary, depositing their offerings on the altar as they left.

By now it had turned dark and lights were on. We had hardly noticed, so transfixed were we by the devotion of the people and by this ancient ritual of prayer and coming together of community that meshes the very fabric of Balinese life.

Slowly, reverently, we too filed out, passing hundreds more walking up the stone steps as we descended. We thanked Didi and her family for their kindness and sadly took our leave, returning to the hotel inspired, opened and hugely grateful for this magnificent experience.

CHAPTER 14

Dateline: Oct 18th 2011

Kuala Lumpur airport… en route to the Phillipines

I am in shock. I just logged onto my email here in Kuala Lumpur airport after a few days internet-free in Bali to discover that a dear friend of mine died tragically yesterday. Kat was statuesque and gorgeous, long dark hair, melting brown eyes and shapely legs, the kind of woman everyone notices when she walks into a room. She hadn't even hit forty...

A police car was chasing another vehicle on Highway 1 and somehow Kat's motorbike got munched in the high-speed chase. The road was closed for seventeen hours while they cleared up the mess. Needless to say, she died instantly.

I first met Kat when she came to my house about eight years ago to see the Maori healers from New Zealand, who come to my house to offer treatments in their traditional healing style. It was a hot day. I remember she was wearing khaki shorts and I admired her legs. We chatted about my jnana yoga group and next thing you know she was joining us on Tuesday nights, driving an hour to be with us, always bringing tasty treats for our potluck supper, often with her daughter, Lauren, in tow.

She quickly became a dear friend. The night of my first book launch party, it was Kat who drove over to pick me up and drop me back home. On party nights she would giggle and cuddle with us all on my oversized couch, radiating joy and grace.

A few years ago she had moved to Middletown to be closer to Harbin and all that it offers. I would often see her

173

on the Harbin sun-deck or in the restaurant and recently had spent quite a bit of time with her and she told me she was thinking of returning to Sacramento and getting involved with our group again.

Alas, it was not meant to be.

As I sit in Kuala Lumpur airport absorbing the shock of this terrible news, everything that seemed important suddenly is not. The small things I was worried about have faded into the background.

I realize it is a privilege to grow old, not a right.

Like lady Diana, Kat will always be remembered as young, sexy and vibrant. But the dreams she and her new husband, Troy, shared for their future, died with her. She will never take that motorcycle trip through South America or see her daughter, Lauren, get married.

More than ever it hits home the importance of living fully in the NOW; appreciating our lives, our bodies, our opportunities, our friends and family. When did you last tell your best friend you love them? Knowing that my dear friend, Kat, will never join me on this scuba diving trip to the Philippines makes me even more grateful to be here in Asia living out my dreams and even more determined to encourage others to do the same.

Kat lived big. She had just returned from South America where she had journeyed with shamans from the Amazon jungles and hiked the mountains of central Peru. She was one to live life to the fullest and she was taken doing something she loved, long hair streaming behind her. riding that motorbike down Highway 1.

I am wondering how to honor her memory. Maybe I will dedicate this book to her... may it be used to inspire people to think bigger, enjoy themselves more and, as Kat did, indulge their passions, so that when that day comes, as it will for all of us, we meet our maker with no regrets, no dreams left unfulfilled, no love unshared.

Chapter 15

Dateline: October 24th 2011
Pura Vida resort, Dumaguete, Phillipines

I am currently in a tropical island paradise leading a yoga and dive vacation. Off the beaten tourist track, we are staying in a small Swiss-run resort called Pura Vida, in Dauin, just south of Dumaguete.

The area is in a sweet stage of development; just a handful of small, boutique resorts scattered along the beach and in-between, the local people are still living as they have for hundreds of years. Looking down from our upstairs restaurant terrace the first morning, I saw a local lady draw water out of her well with an old bucket and scrub her laundry clean on a rock. After, she showered by pouring water over her with all her clothes on, while chickens clucked and crowed all around. No private showers here, no hot water. She and her family did, however, have beachfront property... and a killer view over the bay.

Having just stepped out of a hot shower in my air-conditioned room, about to chow down a scrumptious breakfast of bacon, eggs, pancakes and juices, I felt a twinge of guilt. Although I would by no means be considered wealthy in my own country, in comparison here, I was a millionaire. People here work for a few dollars a day, all with wonderful smiles and such grace, and can only dream of traveling and exploring as I have been blessed to do.

Yet I notice the children run around their island paradise happily, playing with sticks, stones and each other. They may lack material possessions but they more than compensate with imagination, ingenuity and family bonds.

My group is here to dive and I love scuba diving - that

175

feeling of being suspended in the water, free from the constraints of gravity, floating, weightless like an astronaut. I love skimming across glassy, turquoise waters in the early morning sunshine in the dive boat, that first dip into the warm, soft welcoming ocean (you can keep your cold water kelp forests – I like the tropics!). I love the colorful fish and the gorgeous coral reefs, the placid turtles and playful dolphins. It's another universe under the water; alien, potentially dangerous, yet so alluring as to draw me back time after time. Searching out the world's most beautiful underwater landscapes ranks high on my bucket list.

Corals are sensitive animals. They cannot stand much variation of conditions before they bleach and die off. Thirty percent of the world's coral reefs have already been damaged or destroyed by dynamite fishing techniques, pollution, careless divers and warming seas and scientists say that thirty percent more will be damaged in the next twenty years if we do not act soon. I feel a sense of urgency to see as many of them as I can as quickly as possible.

The dive operation here is as easy and convenient as it gets and the sites are world-class. Yesterday we saw turtles, frogfish, a shoal of squid, and multi-colored corals. On one dive, I saw an alien creature. It was about six inches long with a round green body and three bulging purple eyes clustered together on the middle of its head. Our dive master knew where it was hiding and poked his stick into its den so the alien would scurry out. It looked a little alarmed, twitching its lobster-like antennae, encouraging us to go away. Our dive master said it was a flat worm. Well it didn't look very flat to me, unless it was an obese flat worm. After a few minutes of agitated twitching, it reversed itself back into its hiding place in the rock, probably communicating with creatures of its own kind that inhabitants of this planet are unfriendly giants of inferior intelligence.

On that same dive, something else rather odd happened. I had brought my own wetsuit with me. It's quite old and has a tear around the butt area. There I was, intently admiring a lovely piece of coral, when a fish bit my butt

176

through the tear where my red bikini was exposed! I yelled with surprise more than pain, although it did nip me quite hard. Looking around for a culprit, all I saw were innocent looking small tropical fish swimming around. Although I must say, that clown fish looked a bit suspicious. What did he think I was – lunch buffet? I have to assume that the flash of my bikini red attracted the fish. Note to self – wear something other than red in future whilst diving in case larger fish with teeth make the same mistake!

Maybe it was time to fix the hole in my wetsuit. I inquired how I might go about this in the dive shop and they directed me to a cobbler up the street. Gotta love the third world, where poverty is the Mother of invention and creativity – this cobbler could fix anything; shoes, bags... and wetsuits! I left my wetsuit with him overnight and returned the next day to find the hole neatly repaired with a beautifully-fitting patch placed over the tear. That will foil those pesky fish! And my bill? Just $2.50!

It's relaxing for me to dive too and has given me time to think about Kat's passing.

Already I can see a shift in my thinking. I am less concerned about my budget. I am spending more freely rather than worrying about what things cost and being my usual frugal self. Last night I bought a nice bottle of wine for my group and me and ordered lobster. I did it in Kat's honor. She would be the first to encourage us all to enjoy great food and wine. When I get home, I am going to look at all the areas where I have denied myself and start giving myself today what I have put off till tomorrow. I will get the house painted, buy a new dress, invite a friend to a nice dinner out. It's time to loosen those purse strings and live larger, without fear.

Kat's death has made me realize what a huge gift life is. There is a heightened feeling of gratitude for this moment, this body, imperfections and all. I am being kinder to myself – less judgmental, more generous.

I am STILL HERE!

I get to see what's going on in world events. The Libyan

177

leader Gaddhafi was killed today and Libya is celebrating. Children are born, people die, the world goes on. And even as an interested observer, I am happy to be here; to observe the changes in technology, the shifts in societies, the raising of consciousness world-wide.

There is an ancient Chinese blessing, "May you live in interesting times." Well, we do. Even if our own lives suck occasionally, we are still a party to planetary events, even more so now in this interconnected world in which we live.

If I am lucky, I will get to see the next "magic invention", space travel for commoners and free video calls. Oh I forgot – we have SKYPE – we already have that. Sometimes I am just plain curious about "what happens next." Just being alive, I get to witness it all. In light of losing my friend, that alone feels like a great blessing.

Kat's death is inviting me to take stock. Where have I held back from being who I am, from expressing myself as fully as I could? If I died tomorrow would I have fulfilled my own potential? What IS my highest potential anyway?

Where could I be more honest? There are many times when I could be more truthful with people but have often held back so as not to either lose them as a friend or hurt their feelings. What serves the highest potential though? What if my purpose is to help others to see themselves more clearly and I am failing miserably in that process because of my own cowardice and attachment? I resolved to practice being more courageous in my dealings with people in future.

After a day of diving, the spirit feels full from being engulfed in the watery womb of the Mother and the body feels relaxed, a soft tiredness, but tired limbs could use a massage. So after diving one day, I had a massage with Anna, one of the older massage ladies and started to chat to her. She seemed around my age, but it turned out she is just forty-three. Ata, my Maori friend said that in their tribe in New Zealand the women never quite stop bleeding. Her "aunties" still spot at eighty and do not seem to go through menopause like we do. I was curious if this was the case here too. I asked Anna how Filipino women feel about aging and how they deal with menopausal symptoms.

She said she really didn't know as she was still having her periods, but my question must have provoked some inquiry in her, because the next day, she came up to me at the pool waving a piece of paper.

"Miss Julia! I asked three of my friends your questions and I wrote down what they said!"

I examined the crumpled up paper and saw the following written in a scratchy but legible hand:

Not sleep well and much gas in stomach. Sometimes headache.

Feel very angry. Getting hot.

Sometimes cry and feel small.

I asked Anna if these women seek help from a doctor for these matters. She looked surprised.

"Oh no – no doctor. Too much money."

So it's "suck it up and bear it" here in the third world.

Yet these seem to be the happiest people on the planet, always smiling and friendly, joking with each other. During our conversation, Anna said "We live for today. Tomorrow is not here. You think too much."

She's right there. We think too much, we of the western mindset. It's like a disease, spreading inexorably around the world. Now we've got the Chinese thinking too much, even the Brazilians. But not the Filipinos – not yet anyway.

And sometimes we don't think enough.

I did two very stupid things during my week at Dumaguete that could have been avoided with more care. Walking home with the group from a restaurant down the beach without a flashlight, I managed to step into a very hard rock and bang my little toe so badly that it ripped my little toenail almost completely off. That was a new experience! It hurt like a son of a bitch! I yelled loudly and

179

when I got back to my room, I saw that the force of my kick had pulled the nail off at an angle, but it was still hanging by a thread onto my toe. Ow! The slightest pressure on it was excruciating. I can only imagine what Chinese fingernail torture must have been like if this is anything to go by!

The second stupid thing I did was to drink a dodgy tequila sunrise in a local bar in Dumaguete town. Our group was out getting a taste of local culture touring the town and stopped off for a drink and a bite to eat. I ordered a drink and when it arrived on the table, grenadine red and with ice floating, I had an intuition not to touch it. But I didn't listen to myself. I drank it anyway and eight hours later, was overcome with an irresistible urge.... the kind when you do not pass go. You run straight to the nearest bathroom and empty out! Very sexy.

I was sick all night and most of the next day. Luckily, our new Swedish friend, Gita, had some Imodium handy and I gratefully took some. Twenty-four hours later, I was right as rain, a couple of pounds thinner and ready to trip the light fantastic yet again. Just as well, as I was scheduled to take the group to the weekly market the next day.

The market is pretty much like any Wholefoods Market, just without the granola and the yuppies (just kidding!) Small stalls selling locally produced wares for surviving life in the tropics lined the small dirt road leading to the sea. A cacophony of sound, people shouting, pigs squealing and cows mooing filled the air. We learned that a small pig in a sack costs about $40 to $50. Considering the average wage is $50 a month, that seemed quite expensive. However, a small pig will put on about eighty kilos of weight in four months, so it's an investment for the farmer. Gita came with us to the market and had some interesting tales to tell us about the dark side of this idyllic island, that many tourists fail to notice.

A few months ago, a drunk tricycle driver crashed into Sonia, one of our resort waitresses who was on her motor-scooter driving home from work. She hurt her leg really badly and desperately needed surgery, but neither the resort nor her family would help her to pay for it. Forget Government health care, no help there. She suffered badly and was in a lot of pain... until Gita heard about her predicament.

Gita is an avid diver and has been coming to the resort four times a year for the past few years. She is also a schoolteacher back in Sweden. She galvanized her kids to raise money for Sonia's operation. They had bake sales, car wash drives and went door-to-door raising money. The upshot was that Gita came back last time with enough money to pay for the surgery! Sonia got her leg fixed and is recovering. She is still on crutches but the resort has given her an office job and she is healing nicely.

Bless that Gita.

Families are big here. The Catholic Church is alive and thriving here in the Philippines and in Manila I saw large posters of The Pope with "Support Life" written in large letters next to his picture. The Church still wields huge power and family planning is frowned upon. It is not uncommon for women to bear eight to twelve children, which means, of course, that the population has doubled in the last few years and continues to spiral out of control. At least for now, despite being a poor country, there is abundant food and water and you do not see people starving in the streets like you do in India.

If you have a large family of nine or ten and so many mouths to feed, maybe you can sacrifice one of your women for the greater good of the family. At least that is the thinking of many a Filipino Father.

Young girls from fourteen upwards get sent away to the tourist areas by their families to make money the old-fashioned way, in the world's oldest profession. It's prevalent and unavoidable here. There are lots of girly bars and everywhere there are tourists, I see old white guys walking hand-in-hand with some beautiful young Filipina, probably only just legal. The men look at me with scorn. They know what I am thinking. And they are right – I find it somewhat tacky.

These girls do not want to do this. They have been given no choice. They send money home so their Fathers can drink and gamble all day and not have to work. After about ten years, the girls are spent; exhausted, sick, sometimes drug-addicted or riddled with diseases, no longer able to pull clients. Then what does the girl do? She cannot go home. Her presence brings shame to the family. She can get no comfort from the Church, who condemns such actions yet offers few viable alternatives for feeding hungry mouths.

Her best hope is to find a foreigner who will fall in love with her and take her home. That is the big dream for these girls. An escape route out of the hell they are living. For some it happens. Despite poor language skills and little education, many of these women DO find a man to take care of them. He gets young, succulent brown flesh. She gets money, a ticket out, a new start in life. All for sleeping with an older man most western women would not dream of touching. Sorry, but it's true. There are SOME hot younger guys who dabble with the girls, but mostly it's the sad, less-than-desirable older men, balding with beer bellies who chase these women. Maybe they are very nice. I hope so for the sake of these lovely girls who sacrifice their beautiful bodies on the altar of the American dream. Or European, or Australian dream.

At dinner, our group sat near yet another mismatched couple, he around seventy and quite unattractive, she about twenty and beauty queen gorgeous. They hardly spoke. He ordered food for them as she played with her cell-phone. They both looked bored stupid. I hope the sex and the money was worth it.

However, it really was a romantic scene on the beach. The restaurants had put tables out on the beach and lit candles. The lapping waves were maybe five feet away. Fairy lights were entwined around the trees and singers were playing Beatles and John Denver songs. Filipinos are fabulous singers and one guy sounded just like Paul McCartney! The fish was fresh caught and the wine came from Italy, yet my entire bill came to only $6!

182

As I sat looking around, I noticed something. Other than an elderly man selling sunglasses, I had not seen any older local people at the beach or anywhere else in this town for that matter. I asked one of the waiters,

"So where are the older people, over fifty? I don't see any in this town."

"They are all inside. They cannot walk any more. They have bad knees."

"Oh!" I was surprised by his answer. "Can they still work?"

"If they are fishermen or farmers they work. If not their family supports them. I send money to my grandparents."

Hmm. Now I can see the value in the large family. As a childless woman, I had better be keeping my knees good as no grandchild was going to support me.

And I am happy to sleep alone here. After diving I just want an early night and a good night's sleep. Men-on-pause is just fine with me. Divine Mother has filled me to the brim and as I say goodnight to the starry Father sky, I throw myself gratefully on my bed, alone, happy, full.

For once, not thinking too much.

Chapter 16

Dateline: November 15th, 2011
Hong Kong

As the ferry to Lamma chugged further away from Hong Kong Island, the skyscrapers faded softly into the gentle mist, eventually disappearing from sight. The sea-lanes were busy; large cargo freighters on their way to Kowloon docks, other ferryboats plying the seas to Macau or The New Territories, the odd millionaire's pleasure cruiser... I relaxed into my seat, feeling excited to be back in this vibrant, world-class city, anxious to see old friends and to be of service to whomever the universe dropped in my lap.

Half an hour later, punctual as ever, the boat docked smack on time at Yung Shue. Verdant green hills rich with sub-tropical vegetation ringed the bay and small fishing boats bobbed in the waters, a lovely scene, reminiscent of a Greek island, marred only by the power station looming menacingly behind the hill on the left.

Each year, I stop in Hong Kong on the way back from my yoga vacation tours and stay on Lamma Island with my friend Johnny, a world away from the hustle and bustle of Kowloon and Hong Kong Island. It may be just a thirty-minute ferry ride to get here, but it feels like you are moving thirty years back in time. There are no roads here on Lamma, just wide paths, big enough for motorcycles and pushbikes, and perfect for walkers. There is a real sense of timeless island life, quiet and peaceful, in tune with nature.

I get off the boat and start walking to the village, past brightly-lit Chinese sea-food restaurants, each with large tanks of water crawling with live lobsters, crab, squid and fish; The Chinese like their food fresh. Tables are round and set family-style, with a turntable in the middle for dishes that are meant to be shared. It's November, but the weather is warm and muggy and I am wearing shorts like a tourist, sensible walking shoes and a T-shirt. I feel conspicuously unkempt in comparison to the smart local girls and a tinge of envy courses through me as I see them dressed to the nines in the latest fashions - leather pants, high-heeled boots and designer tops. It all looks great on their impossibly slender Asian figures.

The raucous sound of chattering Cantonese-speaking locals fills my ears as I walk past the restaurants. I have another dining destination in mind - the English pub! The great thing about Hong Kong is that because of the many ex-pat Brits and lingering British influence, there are also a number of wonderful British pubs where I can indulge my longing for good British cuisine - and drink!

I head to "The Waterfront" and promptly order myself a pint of cider and a roast lamb dinner. Aahhhh! Heaven! They even have mint sauce to go with the lamb (It's a British thing...), excellent fuel for the walk up to Johnny's house. Johnny's house is not so far away, only ten minutes from the port, but it requires climbing up a very steep hill - a 1 in 5... and today I have a suitcase and bag to lug behind me.

When dinner is over, I walk past the tourist shops selling Indonesian batiks and scarves from China, past the tea and cake shop, resisting the temptation to stop by and eat yet more, turning right at the HSBC bank. I walk through the communal farm area, baby lettuce and spinach in neat rows like tiny green soldiers, past the refuse collection point and the recycle bins, the concrete rain shelter and the community ping-pong table, and on up the hill to Tai Peng village.

Johnny lives opposite the public toilets in Tai Peng village. I mention them because they are actually about the nicest public toilets I have ever seen. Offering a choice of oriental squatter loo or western-style sit-down toilet, they are spotlessly clean and with a convenient roll of toilet paper affixed to the wall as you walk in. There is a nice,

185

clean basin for hand washing and an adequate supply of paper towels. Although I can avail myself of Johnny's very excellent house facilities while I am here, I am nonetheless impressed with Chinese cleanliness and efficiency.

Now please do not get the idea that all public toilets in China measure up to this exacting standard. No Sirree. In fact, the public bathroom that gets my "worst loo anywhere in the world" award is to be found in Guangzhou park, China, where ladies do their business by squatting over a foul-smelling trough through which runs an open sewer. Very unpleasant.

But I digress....

I came here to teach a tantra workshop at a local healing center and John is assisting me. Contrary to popular imagination, a tantra workshop is not some guided, naked orgy romp! In fact, it's a program designed to open and expand the energy field, together with offering tools and techniques for improved intimacy. We keep our clothes on and a safe space is created. I offer a workshop here every year and at the end, there is a line of young women wanting to book me for private counseling sessions. I hear the same old stories time and again – communications between spouses have broken down, sex has petered out into non-existent, the woman feels stuck and miserable, still attached to the outcome of her dreams but unable to navigate through the twisted reality of her current situation.

What they really want is simply someone older to talk to, someone with some life experience who can make sense of what they are going through, who can offer some candid advice about sexuality, relationships, spiritual development; in short, someone with perspective. I have noticed that I must now have that, as it is easy for me to guide them, advise them, give them tools and exercises to develop them and it all seems to work quite nicely.

Vicki came to see me quite distressed. Her husband of three years has stopped having sex with her. She is only thirty-two years old, successful in her career, but feeling like a failure in her marriage. She suspects her husband is

186

cheating on her, but he has denied it. He's says he's not feeling attracted to her anymore. They are both hiding, stuck, unable to confront each other and therefore no longer intimate.

I gave her a list of practical ways to address her issues and personal homework to help her blossom into her feminine radiance, much as Harry would have given me. We talked about what she had learned from her husband and why she felt she had attracted a man with these qualities. When re-framed in this way, she lightened up, saying she could see a possibility of letting go of her attachment to being married "happily ever after." She saw that her own growth and awareness was paramount and if she needed to move on to find the love and intimacy she deserved, so be it. Ultimately, if the measures suggested fail, she will have no choice but to end the marriage before she has children and enmeshes deeper with him.

A theme I saw as a thread running through both the men and women here in Hong Kong is the misguided belief that they do not deserve pleasure. There are a myriad of different religious and cultural values that contribute to the conditioning of children in Hong Kong but the end result is that many people retreat to the safety of their intellect rather than explore the true pleasures of loving intimacy and touch.

As Maria walked into the room to see me, her pain and shame entered the room before her. The tears flowed almost as soon as she sat down.

"I know I'm blocked. I don't want to be anymore. I just can't feel a thing when a man touches me. It's like I want to run and hide inside my head. I just switch off. Then men get frustrated with me and leave. I just don't know how to be any different."

I had no idea when I studied hypnotherapy all those years ago, how useful it would be in these situations. We needed to discover the origin of her issue and hypnotherapy was the best way to do just that. I was able to relax Maria enough to let her drift back in time and tell me about her

187

first sexual experience. She looked surprised as she recalled an uncle touching her inappropriately one day when she was about five years old. She instinctively knew it was wrong. In that moment, she made a decision to take her awareness out of her genitals, to not allow feeling or pleasure in her body. It was a coping strategy as a child, but no longer appropriate for her as an adult.

I took her through a healing of that incident. She spoke her truth to her uncle and communicated with her genitals, welcoming them back onto the playing field of life. She left feeling lighter, cleansed, hopeful for her future with men now that she had re-written her agreement with her body.

I wish I had had a wise auntie or female teacher when I was going through the traumas of my thirties. Of course, I did find Harry. But he was not a woman. He could not share the perspective that an older woman has. How I would have loved to have had a cup of tea and a cozy chat with some open-minded, experienced auntie who had lived her life fully and could offer me the wealth of her life's rich tapestry. Where were my tribal elders when I needed them?

Of course, there was always Oprah. She filled a role for many of us, bringing to light so many women's' issues and discussing them publicly. But those were someone else's problems. Mine were unique and different and I would have cherished a guide at that difficult time of my life.

Now it occurs to me that I am it, I am the go-to older woman for these younger ones. I have not really wanted to think of myself in this way, but here in Hong Kong at least, it is undeniable that this is a role I can play and play well.

In my thirties, I recall how relationships were the be all and end all of my existence. There is, of course, a biological reason for that. We are programmed to repopulate our species, so as a woman, there is a sense of urgency to find a mate and conceive as soon as possible. If that doesn't happen, we get anxious. I remember thinking that if I did not find a man by forty, I would be washed up, on the shelf, over the hill with sell-by date well expired.

When we women are in that space, it's hard for us to

hear that there is plenty of time for men... that the right one will show up bang on time and in the meantime, we get to work on ourselves, we can find joy in all aspects of our lives and allow well-being to settle in.

No. In our thirties, women panic. We often settle for someone not quite suited to us. Maybe we have babies with them, maybe we grow a business with them, as I did, and then, as the misery of incompatibility sets in, we reach out for a mentor, an older woman who can guide us through the minefield of this potentially tricky time of our lives.

The young girls come to me and talk about their marital problems, their sex lives or lack of them, their men, or lack of them. I use my skills as a hypnotherapist to clear blocks that are hampering them and my yogic training to offer tools that will keep them clear and expanded. They leave feeling supported, loved and hopeful. And maybe most important, they leave their shame behind. They dump it in the garbage can as they walk out the door.

I find that shame is the biggest obstacle to the well-being of women, especially in the Chinese and Indian cultures, but we western girls have our fair share too - shame of the failed marriage, shame around the body, shame around sex, shame around not living up to parents' expectations; the list goes on. My job is to reduce their "shoulds" to "goods."

These young ladies think, "things should look different." I say, no, things are OK as they are, all OK, all purposeful. I watch the tension in their knotted foreheads soften and release as they wrap their heads around this new concept of OKness. They may still need to make changes in their lives and act appropriately, but when we understand that everything has a purpose, we can accept our situation in the moment and garner the learning, let go of our resistances to the way things are and make our next move with clarity.

Harry used to say that we are all perfectly poised to learn our lessons, there are no mistakes and there is no such thing as a coincidence. There is the hand of the Divine in all of our lives, guiding us, leading us often into challenging situations in order that we may learn what we do not want, as this is the dimension of contrasts. It's actually useful to experience what we don't want, as then we see more clearly what we do want. It's just that it's hard to see that perspective when we are in the thick of our life dramas.

Maybe that's why I like being fifty. I feel like my dramas have eased off. Everything is smoother, calmer, and more peaceful. It's a time for enjoying and savoring life, rather than stressing out and building up.

Today, my workshop and private sessions over, I am going to relax into that enjoyment, watching the butterflies dance here on Lamma Island. After all, tomorrow I leave this warm paradise and head home to California with winter ahead of me.

When I get back, I think I will start some Internet dating. In fact, I've been writing to some guys through a website while I've been in Asia and a couple of them sound quite interesting. Maybe it's time to start thinking about some male company again....

PART 4

And the fairy waved her magic wand….

Chapter 17

Dateline: November 28th 2011
Dave

My story is ruined. You see, I was supposed to meet the man of my dreams on some romantic beach in Galapagos, ensuring a neat and happy ending to my book like any good romance novel.

But all that changed this week.

Dave found me on *OK Cupid*. He wrote to me whilst I was in Asia. I remember feeling a twinge of excitement when I checked out his profile... Reiki practitioner, massage therapist, a well-known speaker and writer in his field, well traveled and did not suffer fools. Sounded like my kind of guy, even though he had a beard and mustache and I can't stand hairy faces!

He was the first date I arranged after arriving home in the USA.

Dave writes:

After a particularly bad breakup and the resulting months of healing, a friend suggested that it might be time to date. A different friend, much more adept and immersed in the dating "scene" suggested a particular Internet site that would be a good place for more "alternative" type people without simply being an anonymous sex cesspool. I jumped in, wrote words, answered questions, posted pictures and started searching. A short list was created and boldly off to the dating stars I went to go where no man had gone before.

One of the Profiles that made me stop and read was that of a petite blonde English ex-pat who described her

192

work and life mission as a yoga teacher, tantra teacher, world traveler, author and mentor. I would read her words, look at her picture and imagine this diminutive stature, large personality woman living in a world where she would fall for a bear of a man of whom personality was always the thing women have loved and body, well, not so much. A short, eloquent note was sent off to beg the important question.

As it turns out, Yoga Goddess received my note while on an extended teaching trip through Asia. Yet she wrote with an interest and an intention to meet upon her return. A success. Better yet, she wrote a couple more times with trip updates. Even better, when she shared her website address, I discovered that I had actually seen her before when searching Google for yoga teachers in my area and somehow felt I knew her.

It was in that moment that a rush of understanding came to me. As a Body and Energy Worker I know this feeling. But it is often affirmed or corrected when I touch someone. Can't touch her in Asia, so I was content with a warm fuzzy feeling. As far as I was concerned, her return couldn't come quickly enough. Every "coffee date" in the meantime, good or bad, always left me wondering about the 'free spirited one'.

"Hi Julia, I'm Dave. Great to meet you. Can I get you a coffee?"

We were in my local Starbucks. I saw a giant of a man standing before me, well dressed, imposing but 6 ft 5 huge and broad to match. He had to be at least four hundred pounds.

"Thanks – I'll have a tall latte and one of those yummy caramel bites – I am totally addicted to them!"

I was nervous and babbled, feeling a bit awkward and self-conscious as I felt Dave's big blue eyes scanning me for the first time.

We found a couple of comfy seats and started chatting;

193

small talk about my Asia trip, what he does for a living and the usual stuff we do whilst our minds evaluate the person we are meeting and our energies meet and sense the other.

"He doesn't look like his picture," I was thinking. "He's way bigger, has less hair and looks older."
But I LOVED talking to this man! I instinctively felt safe with him, and after feeling ungainly and clumsy from being around delicate, elegant Asian women, in Dave's presence I felt petite and feminine, a good feeling for me.

Dave said he was an agronomist, an expert on grass and turf and works with golf courses. Jack Nicklaus employed him for years to help build golf courses all over the world. He'd traveled as much as myself. Yet as a true Renaissance man, Dave also played bass in a band, loved to cook, dance and go to hot springs; and dive.

"I love to touch and learned massage at Esalen Institute a few years ago. If you'd like me to come over and work the jet lag out of you I'd be happy to offer."

Well, really, a very nice man wants to practice his massage on me. He was fluent in that smooth, flowing Esalen-style technique that is so relaxing to receive. What girl in her right mind would say no to that?

Besides I really LIKED this man, even though I did not feel attracted to him in a physical way. I was happy to get to know him better as a friend. Of course, I did not say that right away. That would be off-putting. So we made a massage date for the following week and said our goodbyes.

Dave writes:

Upon the return of Lady Julia, we agreed on a time and a place to hold the ritual ceremony of The Coffee Date. It's not a hard activity if you like job interviews, root canals and other invented activities that are designed as emotional spanking machines.

I'm a wreck all day with nerves yanking my system like

194

several hundred bee stings. And at the same time, I have a feeling of peace like I'm meeting an old friend. In the weeks waiting for her return, I'd had a few of these first dates and a couple of second dates and for the most part dating was starting to look and feel like an activity along the lines of stacking deck chairs on The Titanic.

Miss Julia entered the Starbucks, late, but not too late. She had told me she'd be the girl in jeans and a pink jacket. There were jeans, no pink jacket; a sign she was just checking the box and meeting 'The Large American' to get it over with?

The most important thing to me, immediately, was that her vibey, intelligent speech was real and profound and I found myself falling into her British accent as if I had just tried to walk across a swift moving stream. Plunging into the exhilarating cold, realizing I had to swim in the current of the conversation with all I had, exhilarated, yet somehow forgetting I never intended to swim.

Time passed quickly. I simply had to ask her if I could see her again. She related that there were some busy moments, but there were some openings. I figured I could take that. But my overarching sense was that she really didn't see me.

Coffee dates. Had me thinking that what I should do is just take my dog and head for the hills somewhere. Reminds me of a scene in Robert Redford's classic movie, 'Jeremiah Johnson', wherein Redford's character asks the old mountain man, Grizz, if he ever got lonely for a woman.... a full time night woman. The answer was something to the effect of him having traded in his squaw for a gun and some tobacco. Wisdom? Perhaps.

Here's what I knew: a Goddess stepped into my life and I recognized it. As a man, regardless of my height, weight, education, cultural construct or anything else that makes me the special creation I am, I owe it to myself to embrace that recognition enough to show this person who I am. Once she sees and I know her vision is clear, then and only then, if she doesn't feel chemistry... the credits roll, a sad song begins to play and this cowboy rides away.

That's not how it happened.

A few days later, Dave appeared at my door with a table, clean sheets, delicious smelling massage oil and a big smile on his face. I could tell he was nervous as he set up the table in my living room, doing his best to make me feel that I was in good hands, with a professional, clinical attitude.

"Come and lie down face-up," he said. "Here, I'll cover you up nice and warm with this blanket." I hopped on the table and he laid his hands on me – large, healing hands, energy pouring through them. I relaxed immediately. Oh I'm in heaven!

The large, confident hands glided effortlessly over my body, kneading out knotty kinks and relaxing tight muscles, still sore from sitting on planes. We didn't talk much. Other than checking on the pressure for me, he encouraged me to let go and relax deeply.

It's rare I can drop into a deep, open space whilst being massaged by someone new. Normally I need a little time to learn to trust my therapist, I need to feel safe in order to open my energy fully. But with Dave, I felt totally protected and safe and quickly fell into a state of bliss. That surprised me.

Who is this guy?

When he finished, he sat and held my feet, dropping into that float zone with me, merging energy for a moment.

I sat up slowly, thanking him as he started to pack up his gear. "Let me make you a cup of tea," I offered, wanting to give something back to this lovely man.

"I'll take it the English way. Black tea with milk," said Dave, who it turns out, had lived a few years in England and can understand my odd transatlantic expressions and slang.

We sat on my couch sipping tea and chatted warmly. That night I was having a gathering for Kat with some of the people from my jnana group who knew her when she was a member. My friend Kathy was coming early to spend some time with me. Dave and I were still engrossed in conversation when she knocked on the door.

"Come in, sweetie, and I'll make you tea. Here come sit on the couch with Dave. He'll give you a hug if you need one."
I brazenly volunteered his loving arms.

While Kathy poured out her heart and sorrow over Kat's passing, she sat between Dave and I, both our arms around her. It felt so right to be here comforting one of my best friends with a man I hardly knew.... I was cognizant of the strong, masculine space Dave held; quiet, loving, present. I liked that. It's a rare gift to be able to comfort someone with pure presence alone, but his energy was doing exactly that on that sad day when we were mourning the loss of our friend.

Still, much as I liked and appreciated this lovely man, I had been with a large man before and had sworn to only date fit, healthy men. Plus he had that hairy face.

No. I just couldn't do it - there is NO way I am kissing a guy with a mustache.

Dave writes:

I've studied bodywork and energy-work all over the world as a way to improve my health and as a way to help others. When my father passed away in 2003, I took it much more seriously. I was the standout student in every class I took and as a way to heal and as a form of exercise I took every opportunity I could to give work -chair massage at sporting events, working a few hours a week at several day spas, eventually opening my own healing studio and teaching. Along the way I became a Reiki Practitioner and helped develop an integrated hot/cold stone treatment combined with Reiki technique. I even offered massage for the USA Olympic Athletes in Beijing. Safe to say that I'm confident in this arena, which is why I'm giving my bodywork resume.

I found myself offering massage to Lady Julia in the hope that I could get to know her better via my touch senses and that the same would transfer for a shot at a happy ending. (Get your mind out of the gutter - not "that" kind of happy ending wherein Mama Kim will love you long time.) Julia, being a seasoned healing arts person, gladly accepted and a 2:30 in the afternoon time was chosen. She said she had a table and linens and all that, but I had mine handy, just the same. After a quick chat, she produced the world's oldest, pink colored massage table. Well used but would do the job. I had my lotion of choice ready and we talked about pressure and injuries past and all that clinical stuff. On the table she went.

Up to this point I was relatively composed. After thousands of massages I should be.

And then I touched her. I've been searching for the words to describe this initial feeling and the best that seems to come has something to do with being plugged into one of those huge power turbines they have at the base of Hoover Dam. I've never been connected to one of them, but I now know what it might feel like it. The smallish Brit nearly knocked me off my feet with her strong energy flow and I began to sweat and shake as if I had had twelve shots of espresso. I don't remember much, but somehow I managed to make my way through some flowing work and a bit of deeper work, using about 30 percent of my pressure potential. Of course she commented on liking pressure, but I was not about to mess up by going too far.

We had our first small connection as she curled into a ball on the table after the massage and we talked a moment. It was the first time she had let her guard down, as if one of those fuzzy-hatted Buckingham Palace guards finally cracked a smile. I felt encouraged, then later foolish, as I learned from her that she had studied massage herself before moving on to higher pursuits. For sure, I could have run some deeper work and for sure she must have known I

198

was a nervous wreck. We shared a cup of tea and some small talk with her taking a position as far away as possible from me as we sat on the couch with our tea.

Massage adventure over, I sent a note of thanks with a very open-ended invitation to get together. Her reply caught me off-guard...

The next day, I woke up thinking about Dave. I liked him, I really did, but I was still not feeling really attracted in a physical way. I wrote him a note that said as much. "Dave – I really love our friendship and look forward to getting to know you better. But I don't sense a romantic attraction with you."

There it was; crisp, honest and short.

But Dave was not to be deterred. He wrote back in an email shortly after, admitting that he had a huge crush on me. I had guessed that and was not quite sure what to do about it, but it's so rare I meet anyone as fascinating as Dave. I wanted to keep a door open for a friendship at least.

"Lets go see a movie together," he suggested. We'd talked about seeing "J. Edgar" and arranged another date.

And so it came to pass that Dave took me to the movies.

There was something different about him when I saw next... he looked more handsome to me, but it took me a while to figure out why - he had shaved! All that was left was a small amount of hair on his chin. The rest was history. I complimented him on looking younger, not hiding behind the hair. He really did look tons better.

We saw the movie sitting next to each other but not touching, not holding hands. I felt comfortable beside him but was not feeling any desire for more closeness. Mutual enjoyment of the movie was feeling like plenty for me.

Afterwards, we went for a drink at The Elephant Bar. Drinking a mojito and having yet more sparkling conversation, I looked at him a little more deeply and felt a twinge of interest in my body, the beginnings of an attraction. Maybe I should look more deeply here. What if there was something here for me and I could not see the wood for the trees, colored as my judgment of him was by my former experiences with large men in my life. During the course of conversation I discovered he had played golf on seven continents, putted with Bill Clinton at The White House, and was clearly a well-read, highly intelligent person. Not a run-of-the-mill man, this one. I was intrigued, but still resistant.

We walked back to his truck and as we parted, I leaned over and gave him a quick peck on the lips - soft lips, nice. I jumped out of his truck making no future plans, remaining non-committal. I thanked him for the lovely evening and drove home, noticing a warm feeling inside me.

Dave writes:

We both had expressed an interest in seeing the movie about J. Edgar Hoover and so after a bit of schedule syncing, a time and place was suggested and agreed and we met at the appointed moment. She looked much more beautiful that I had remembered and the truth was I was really taken by her whole vibe. She picked perfect seats and we chatted and commented through the previews and settled into a good movie. Her energy was all around me and it felt nice, but when I would steal a glance, her body language was very closed. Sitting far away from me again. The possibility of some "date type" contact as benign as holding hands didn't seem any more possible than Lady Gaga calling me for music lessons. Nonetheless, we both enjoyed the movie and keyed in on the same interesting parts.

We had talked about having a drink after the show and picked a place. I was rather shocked when she offered to jump in my vehicle, declaring that she trusted me. "Am I getting through to this woman?", I thought. Perhaps, but still she sat as far away from me as possible. We had a really enjoyable conversation over a nice yummy cocktail and I felt happy to have so much to talk about with her. Our combined world travels would certainly fill three books and we both had some cool stories to tell. I felt warm and wonderful.

As we left to walk to my car, I had the urge, once again, to just hold her hand. As I looked for the possibility, Miss Julia, hands in pockets, was walking far enough away that my hand would never reach her. Not that into me. I get it. But at the same time we were having this great mental and spiritual connection. During our drink I had told her about my Stone Reiki work, so we revisited this subject quickly as a possibility for further connection. She leaned over, gave me a peckish kiss that only a sister could give a brother and off she went.

Here's what I wrote in an email that night:

Wonderful evening with you. Thank you so much. What a blessing you are.

I'm sure you can tell I have a crush on you. Not really sure how to handle myself with that. Kind of a new thing. Usually I'm the one who isn't feeling it. I find myself giving you lots of space when I actually want to be close.

Advice? ... since you are the oracle.

Here's what she wrote back:

Good morning!

I am enjoying getting to know you very much - I feel very comfortable with you. How wonderful you are feeling things...can you celebrate the feeling without any attachment to outcome??
(I know - that's a hard one...)

You must be in my psychic space because I dreamed about you last night.
Anyway I am remaining open.

Love J

Can I celebrate the feeling....? Sure Julia, just like I can celebrate Salsa by looking at a Tomato and a couple of chillies. I get what she was saying and I know this was a stretch for her, but I'm not the sort of man who doesn't step to a challenge. And really, isn't meeting someone who makes me feel this way enough to celebrate? Doesn't that make for a stitched deep sense of love? Perhaps I'm just a damn sap who should be ghost writing romance novels for lonely ladies in Florida to read by the pool. Or perhaps I need to shave my head, don the robes and train German shepherds with Monks of New Skete and never speak to another human female again. Confused and passionate, it was time to take the 1 iron out of the bag and execute a low screamer into the wind, pin high to win the match.

My reply was perhaps one of the bravest things I have ever written:

Someone told me once that we put up walls not to keep people out, but to see who cares enough to break them down. And I think that goes hand in hand with getting what you need, but not always what you think you want.

I'm glad I found my way into your dream space. You've been speaking in mine since first writing from Asia.

You are special, Lady Julia. So am I. So when you ask if I can celebrate, it makes me laugh because there is already a celebration.

"Piglet sidled up to Pooh from behind. "Pooh?" he whispered.

"Yes, Piglet?"

"Nothing," said Piglet, taking Pooh's hand. "I just wanted to be sure of you."
— A.A. Milne, Winnie-the-Pooh

I hope your day has surrounded you with love. Today your words surrounded me with special. Thank you.

After I pressed the 'send' button on this beauty, I felt nothing but strength and peace. In my life, I've often been unable to be strong enough in my own voice. This was strong, loving language and I knew that it was determined, but not rude or pushy. I didn't want a "take it or leave it" kind of thing. And I didn't want to be one of those guys who related that they weren't looking for friendship. I simply and totally wanted to make sure I had been seen and for the most part, didn't feel like that had happened yet.

I had made the offer to put my stones to work on Julia and was excited to hear the answer. In the mean time, I kept sending her daily inspirational quotes. The reply came quickly and we set a time. She insisted on feeding me dinner on a Sunday evening and with the Reiki to follow. Perfect. Perhaps my stones could do great work and I could relax into her buttery smooth accent, yet once more.

More quotes followed. I felt I was being wooed.

He had told me of his stones, his connection with the stone people, how the stones when laid out on the body will relax and heal the muscles and energy centers. That sounded very appealing and I was intrigued. I wrote and asked to feel the stones.

Sunday December 18th

Take 2. Dave at my door with table, sheets, stones and stone heater. This time, I cooked dinner for him first. I'm not a great cook but I make a mean buffalo bolognaise. Dave was appreciative and we dined well. The feeling between us was relaxed, fun.

Then he set up the table and laid out the hot stones, laying them under me, on me, placing small ones between my toes, large ones in each hand, running reiki energy through my energy field. I was GONE! It relaxed me so deeply, my spirit went to some far away corner of the universe to play with the angels. Once again, I was blissed out and happy. In the zone.

Who IS this man?

When we were finished with the healing treatment, I lay on the table for a while still bathing in the delicious energy, still feeling his field merged with mine. I didn't want to disconnect from that and could tell he was being polite and awkward about what to do next. I needed to know how it would feel to get a little closer, so I took the reins.

"Dave, would you be willing to cuddle me on the couch?"
He didn't need to be asked twice!

We moved over to the couch and I laid myself on top of this giant of a man, and let his arms unfold me. Oh he was SO comfortable! I nuzzled my head against his gigantic neck and settled in, softening. We lay there, still, hardly moving, till 2:00 a.m. in the morning, letting our stories pour out. Talking, sharing, enjoying each other. But not once did I kiss him. No sirree, I was still in the confusion; confused I was starting to feel attracted to this very large man, not sure yet about taking it any further.

At last, I kicked him out, but invited him back, to join our jnana group on Tuesday.

Dave continues:

Julia, The Stone Treatment

This little one plays it so cool. I've been sending my daily meditative quotes to her and she always comments but doesn't say too much. But this time it is different and she came right out and just asked when I was coming to give her my 7 Stones Treatment. Signs of being much more free. We quickly set up a date and time and I sent the usual speech about Do's and Don'ts for this powerful treatment. She offered to do dinner and I didn't want to say yes partly because I didn't want her to go to any trouble and partly

204

because I don't usually eat before doing this work. It is intense and I don't like the feeling of any energy going to my digestive system when my other systems need to be engaged. But she really wanted to and because of the time of day, it really made sense.

Dinner was amazing. She did a wonderful rice pasta (we are both into largely gluten free eating) and this really strong sauce that only needs a couple of tweaks to be world class. She says she's a simple English cook, but I think there is more foodie there than she admits. Dinner over, I offer to help clean up, but she makes quick work of it and I'm busy setting up my stone warmer and gear. What is cool is that she is REALLY up for this. She doesn't do much in the way of asking questions, she just wants to get to the experience and that makes me happy.

My "7 Stones Reiki" treatment is pretty special and was learned from a true master and adapted to fit my style. I use a combination of Colorado Basalt (Black) heated stones and Colorado Marble (white) cool chakra stones. The idea is to sandwich the victim in-between hot upwardly radiating energy and cool earth seeking energy. Temperature is critical and the hot stones can be really hot, but I back off to a safe temperature and go with my feelings. She's a high-energy person and my intuition says that the cold stones are really the most key thing. I put Julia face up with a spinal layout below her and begin to tuck in pairs of dark stones under joints and key points. Two "flight control" stones are placed in her hands and some small toe stones are put between her toes, which she says immediately that she loves. The seven Chakra stones in the form of animals, drums, etc are placed on top of her and immediately she relaxes into the weight of the large cold stones. It's my job just to be the cruise director and let the gang of Stones, Spirits and Ancestors do the work. A guided meditation begins and I run symbols and the Reiki energy kicks in hard. This one is a receptor. For the next forty-five minutes she receives, hard and I watch the flow and colors change and I'm sweating like a banana farmer in a monkey sanctuary because everything about this woman is big big big. Big like no one who has ever been on my table. I'm overwhelmed.

The stones quickly accomplish the work and when the flow is perfect and my touch yields balance it is time to start taking off stones and bring her back to life. Simple. I'm out of the way. It's not me and I know this and that makes my nerves feel better.

The next event was a bit of shocker to me. As I get her up and bring her to the now, she asks me if I'd lie down on her big davenport sized couch and "cuddle" with her... "have a cuddle" was how she put it. We simply and quickly fell onto the couch as if we had been doing this forever; a little talk and a lot of chill and I remember touching her hair and kissing her on the top of the head as if to say, "relax, I'm OK". She did. There wasn't really a romantic moment. It was more of a spiritual thing and she talked about how she felt and what was important to her at the moment. So much in "the now". So awesome.

Before I knew it, it had become very late and I was totally exhausted. Packing up my gear wasn't very easy. It seemed like I was in a haze. Driving home seemed to take forever and I remember very little beyond that.

The next day I sent a heartfelt thank you:

Thank you for a lovely dinner. For a lovely time. For a chance to bring my gifts.

You are confused about me. I get it. Don't be. We have something to explore. Could surprise us both, I think.

Blessings.

-Dave

To which the reply came quickly:

Good morning!

So I slept well and hard - for six wonderful hours and

206

woke at 8:00 a.m. feeling very refreshed. How about you?

A lovely night... and as an intrepid explorer I say yes.

Your move...

J

That following morning I woke up with Dave on my mind. I could not shake it. He stayed with me that whole day, that night and the following morning, as though I was being stealthily courted on some other plane. His energy somehow visiting me on the etheric level, getting inside of me, battling down my resistance.

Tuesday morning I woke up excited about the evening. I think I had already decided to go to the next level, in fact, couldn't wait.

In jnana group that week we were working on self-forgiveness. I knew Dave had some of that work to do and thought it would be great for him to see what I do with groups, but I had already told him I do not sleep with my students. So I wrote to him that day and said that I wanted him to come and insisted he came as my guest as otherwise it changed the rules of the game. I guess that gave him a message. I was starting to open!

At 7:15 p.m., Dave's massive frame filled my doorway. My heart jumped and I noticed I was really pleased he'd shown up. Others followed and at 7:30 p.m., we sat in a circle on the floor and began group. I asked Dave to sit next to me and took his hand in mine as we did the opening meditation together. It felt good, warm and strong.

During group, I could feel him paying big attention to what was being shared. He had told me that personal growth was important to him and it pleased me to see him engaging fully in the jnana yoga processes.

When group was ended, people left and we returned to the couch. I call it my magic couch as once you have sunk into it, it's very hard to get off! And this time as I lay myself down next to this powerful man, I did kiss him.

Again and again... deliciously, slowly, quickly, allowing myself to open my energy more and more to his strong, masculine presence. I came up for air and lifted my head.

"Listen, I have to tell you, my ex thinks I am bossy, opinionated and demanding."

"I love a girl who knows her own mind."

"I'm a terrible cook and for a domestic Goddess you'd better look elsewhere."

"I loved your food the other night. But luckily for you, I LOVE to cook. My Dad was a trained cordon bleu chef and taught me everything he knew."

"I travel a lot. I'm gone for weeks every year."

"Well absence makes the heart grow fonder. Or I'll join you."

Well OK then. I'm testing this man, pushing his limits and he eats my words and spits them right back out. All in his stride.

With that he put his lips back on mine and we kissed again, for another couple of hours...

The deal was sealed.

Julia, The Group

My move? Really? She actually granted that kind of licence? Amazing. I played it cool and suggested a few openings in my schedule and bravely mentioned my plan to go to Wilbur Hot Springs for a soak later in the week.

Her response was a very clear invitation to join her Yoga Circle held every Tuesday night to see her in action. I was honored and really wanted to come. Plus it just seemed like the right thing to do. I inquired about what to say to the "how do you know Julia" question which had already been thrown at me on Massage Night by an arriving friend who needed comfort. She answered with integrity. "Just tell them we have had a couple dates". Simple. In the meantime our email chats flowed.

I arrived to her Tuesday group not knowing what to expect and also knowing it was the perfect place for me. She greeted me warmly and I figured out right away that she wasn't going to hide the fact that she liked me in front of her friends and clients. This is really such an honoring thing for a new person on someone's radar and I was overjoyed. The group was dynamic and amazing and I soaked it up. She's a great teacher and leader and I would be a fool not to recognize that she was now my teacher. Can I date my teacher? Sure. Of course. I need great teachers and can separate the two. It's not like some Van Halen song or teen boy fantasy. I just think a man has to recognize the idea that a woman can be honored in her majesty without the man's loss of ego. Julia Tindall is damn good at what she does and I could learn from her. Romantic possibilities aside, this is a truth.

Maybe she knew it and maybe she just did it, but Julia did two things to seal the deal with me on that particular point. First, as the group got into circle, she made a place for me right next to her. As a new guest, I felt welcomed. As a potential "man", I felt special, my energy soared. Second, after the final Om's, she came and sat next to me and put her arm around me. I had seen her be affectionate with others, but in this instance, it was more than that. She claimed me. Marked her territory. Showed everyone in the room that I was important to her. My fragile male ego drew immediate strength from this. I was to be counted. I mattered. I'll tell you, that, ladies, is how to win a man. Win. Win. Win. I was high as Everest Base Camp in that moment. As I milled about afterwards, meeting and talking with others, I felt her eyes on me, checking on me. She would sometimes breeze by and touch me. Perfection.

As people left, she made sure that I knew I was to stay and once the last person closed the door we fell, nay we nearly leapt onto her Magic Couch and melted into each other's arms. Moments later our lips found what I knew I desired (and as it turns out so did she) and I was kissed the kiss of a lifetime. Just writing about it turns me into a shivering yarn ball of nerve endings. That kiss, the most perfect of my forty-five years on the human stage was so very potent in meaning and depth that whatever pain I had over relationships past went headlong into the void never to be returned. My friend, if you are reading this and have not been healed by a kiss, I feel for you. It cannot be better.

There were words exchanged. Some fool effort to try to get me to see her flaws. I was having none of it. We kissed, for hours that night, well into the wee predawn of the following morning and I knew then that regardless of how or what the future would bring, my life had just changed. Forever. It's not a sappy Fabio-covered book. It's the ultimate desire of my heart to have real and spectacular romance.

Here, with this small woman of gigantic power it came when least expected and most needed.

PART 5

GALAPAGOS

Chapter 18

Dateline: February 1st, 2012
En route

It was dark and raining at 4:30 a.m. as we pulled up to the curbside at Sacramento International airport. I sleepily grabbed my bag and leaned over to give Dave a kiss.

"Have a wonderful time and don't worry about me. I'll miss you but I'll be fine," he said, a little unconvincingly.

"I'll miss you too, but the month will fly by and before you know it, I'll be home."

I looked deeply into his eyes, fearing that this lengthy separation would be hard on him. I was going towards the trip of a lifetime. He was staying home in rainy Sacramento with a heavy workload and a hole in his free time now that I would no longer be there to monopolize his every free moment.

We had been pretty much inseparable for the last few weeks, catching up on ninety-nine combined years of life. To our great mutual joy, we had found ourselves amazingly compatible in almost every way. We enjoyed the same foods, both appreciated the same restaurants and had the same taste in movies, so going out together was easy, smooth and fun. Dave was such a competent, in charge kind of man that he allowed me to relax into my feminine nature, trusting his decisions. He quickly learned my likes and dislikes and soon knew exactly what would surprise and delight me the most.

He also loved my community, especially who he called my "mystical women," the friends of mine who were energy workers sound healers or meditation teachers in their own right. He reveled in getting to know my large group of friends and students, joining in with the jnana groups, proud of the work I did with people, even encouraging his own friends to join us. In short, he fit right in with my lifestyle and I, in turn, got to receive the blessing of his love and support.

We locked lips one more delicious time.

Yum. I'll never tire of Dave kisses... but the 6.00am flight to Houston was boarding shortly and it was time to go.

It was a little hard to believe I was actually taking a trip just for myself. Normally when I travel I am meeting a group and guiding a tour. This time, it was just for me, like in the old days, when I would pack my trusty backpack, hop a flight somewhere sunny and disappear for a few months. Except that my old backpack would no longer fit my needs! Instead I had bought a nifty, new and larger roller bag that converts into a backpack for walking up flights of stairs or boarding boats. As I picked it up out of Dave's truck, I hoped those occasions would be few and far between – this puppy was heavy! Still I had managed to stuff all required clothing for both tropical and mountain weather plus my dive gear into the bag. That plus a small daypack and passport purse and I was set to go and as mobile as possible.

In my thirties, I traveled way lighter! No bag of supplements needed then, no computer, ipod or headphones to lug around. A camera was my only nod to electronics in those days and a bottle of Lomotil for possible tummy upsets, my only medicine. Still I was only bringing one bag and no extra baggage fees applied.

I had mixed emotions as I watched Dave drive off. On the one hand, this was a trip I had dreamed of my whole life... I had worked hard to make the money to afford it and had spent all year preparing to take this month off. My life set in order, bills paid and classes put on hold, it was a precious time out for me, away from my usual obligations and teaching schedule.

But after meeting Dave, the last few weeks had felt like a whirlwind. I hadn't even had time to think much about the

213

trip, just arranging the most basic necessities of a hotel in Quito and a time and place to meet up with Janice, my friend who was joining me. I felt sad to leave my man after so short a time together, but we both agreed it was best for me to go for the whole time as planned. He would be there when I got home and I would return richer for the experience.

I walked over to Continental Airlines to check in, got on the plane and slept most of the way to Houston, having had only about three hours sleep the night before. On arrival my body started to wake up and demand food. Now as airports in the USA go, Houston ranks as one of the better ones as far as choice of dining establishment. I settled on a Deli where the food looked at least somewhat real and fresh and deciding on a chicken salad roll, proceeded to engage in ordering said item with Audrey.

Audrey looked like she had just eaten a lemon. Short, chubby, with orange hair, black skin and an attitude, I doubt this was Audrey's dream job when she left school and truth be told, she would probably have rather been elsewhere at 11am on a Wednesday morning than in an airport helping frazzled customers. Still, it would have helped if I could have understood her!

"I'd like the chicken salad sandwich please on a roll."

"Would you like matoes, picks, onjuns and letts with that?"

"What?"

'Would you like matoes, picks, onjuns and letts with that?"

"Oh... yes tomatoes and lettuce only please. No pickles or onions."

"You want may and must?"

"I'm sorry, what did you say?"

"You want mayo and mustard?"

"Oh... yes just a little please."

214

"Wanna tata salad or yogit as a side?"

"Pardon, I didn't quite catch that?"

"Tater salad or yogurt as a side?"

"Oh... I'll have the potato salad please."

Oh God, please let that be the last decision I have to make...

Audrey probably thought I was yet another buffoon foreigner who spoke lousy Texan. I was glad to get out of there and nurse my sandwich in the dining area away from her scathing eyes.

Continental Airlines had boasted of a meal on board the next leg of my journey to Panama, being a posh international flight and all that. However experience has taught me to be mistrustful of the culinary delights of American airlines.

I was not wrong.

When "lunch" was served, I bravely chose the chicken wrap. The stewardess handed me some foul concoction of bean paste mashed up with a meat that only vaguely resembled anything familiar, served with an iceberg lettuce salad complete with high calorie dressing and zero nutrition. Thank God I had eaten beforehand. Thanks be to Audrey.

Still, all was not lost. After a mere four hours, we landed in Panama and transferred to a Copa Airlines plane for the short flight to Quito, capital of Ecuador. A snack was served consisting of REAL unadulterated turkey meat in a tasty sandwich and as much free wine as I could put away in two hours, which by then was quite a lot. Yes, even this two-bit Panamanian airline could serve recognizable food and decent Chilean vino. And people wonder why American airlines lose money...

I took advantage of being cooped up in a flying tin can to open my "Lonely Planet Guide to Ecuador." The great news is, there are tons of exciting places to visit after our Galapagos trip and I can't wait to see them all! Rainforests,

215

old colonial cities, laid-back beach resorts on the Pacific coast.... we will be spoiled for choice... and Quito, as a designated UNESCO world-heritage site, sounds amazing.

A little later we landed.

"Welcome to Guayaquil," the stewardess said over the loud speaker.

Guayaquil? Surely she must be mistaken? We are in Quito.

"Due to bad weather, we cannot fly safely into Quito airport. Please take your personal belongings and disembark. We will try again to fly to Quito in another hour."

Ah shucks. These things always happen when we are the most tired.

I got off the plane with all the other passengers and spent an hour wandering around the terminal lounge. It felt good to stretch my legs but, my gosh, I surely could have used some shut-eye.

An hour later we were all back on board as rain pounded down outside. We took off for Quito. After about an hour, I felt the plane start to descend. Then the captain came on the intercom:

"We are so sorry, but the visibility in Quito has once again deteriorated to less than a kilometer and we cannot land. We are heading back to Guayaquil."

A collective groan echoed through the cabin.

By then I was so punch drunk tired I was beyond feeling any resistance to the situation. Anyway there was absolutely nothing to be done except surrender to the fact that I was still sitting on an airplane.

We landed… and sat there whilst the pilot negotiated on our behalf. Eventually we all disembarked again but this time, went through passport control and got on a bus that took us to a hotel. It was 5:45 a.m. I had been traveling for twenty-four hours solid. Thank God I was about to lie flat and get sleep! Good night!

Chapter 19

Dateline: February 2nd, 2012
Quito, Ecuador

"Welcome, Julia!" said Bernice as I climbed the stairs to my guesthouse in Quito. "We stayed up till 3:00 a.m. waiting for you last night, then figured you were not coming. I'm glad to see you made it today."

I had finally arrived in Quito at 4:00 p.m. after a leisurely morning sleeping in at our Guayaquil hotel. At lunchtime we had all been herded back onto the plane for the forty-minute flight to Quito, this time arriving in lovely, clear weather, affording a great view of the mountains surrounding this high Andean capital.

"Coffee and tea are available all the time and we serve breakfast here in the morning," continued Bernice. "There is a video library and TV upstairs, so make yourself at home and enjoy your stay."

Bernice is a lovely Swiss lady and the wife of Jorge, an Ecuadorian. Together they offer European hospitality with a South American flair in the restored house they call Villa Nancy. They opened it as a guesthouse a few years ago. The price for a single room? $22 a night!

I unpacked some essentials and ran out to ask Jorge about a travel agency I had read about online that specializes in last-minute Galapagos cruises. A decent cruise is horrendously expensive and Janice and I had trusted that the right boat would present itself at a bargain price. I needed to go and nail down our cruise immediately. Our flights were booked to leave to the islands in two more days!

"It's only five minutes walk from here. I'll take you there myself," offered Jorge, my   charming host.

218

A few minutes later, we were at the agency, picking up tickets. A first class boat had some spaces open and it looked very nice. We ended up paying hundreds of dollars less than if we had booked in advance from the USA. Sweet.

Janice had emailed to say she was still stuck in Guayaquil, as her flight from Miami had run into the same issue and had also diverted. Her pilots had needed a sixteen-hour break before they could legally fly again. She hoped to arrive at 1:30 a.m! I had the evening to myself and was itching to explore the old town of Quito and discover more about its rich history.

I wrapped up warm as the mountain air at this altitude was bound to cool down once the sun set and took a taxi to the main square in the old town.

What a sight greeted me.... a gorgeous Spanish-style plaza tastefully illuminated with old-style lighting, all the better to highlight the charming old buildings that surround the square. It looked like it had been transported brick by brick from Europe.

In the sixteenth and seventeenth centuries, those Spaniards did an amazing job at bringing their architects and building techniques over to The New World and many of the original buildings remains wonderfully intact. UNESCO declared Quito a World Heritage Site and I can see why. There is a charm to the city that is both elegant and inviting.

I noticed something else. A few years ago, I had gone to Peru to visit the high Andean city of Cuzco and the ruins of Machu Pichu. The main square in Cuzco stank of urine. On the contrary, here, delicious cooking smells assaulted my nostrils as I wandered around, reminding me it was time to eat my first Ecuadorian meal!

When in a brand new country, it can pay to follow a guidebook's recommendations. I have always been a fan of Lonely Planet Guide books, having used them as my travel bibles in Asia in the early eighties. They have excellent maps and are written by travelers for travelers, detailing all

219

the things you need to know such as which hotels best suit your budget and where to find a restaurant with ambience near the grand plaza in Quito.

I was directed to a small, obscure entrance, which opened to steps descending to a cave below. This restaurant was the kind of place you would never just stumble upon. Some Lonely Planet researcher had found it, however, and now I got to enjoy its candlelit cavernous vibe and a hearty lamb stew; with a decent class of Chilean cabernet to wash it down … aaahh! I had arrived!

After dinner, I continued my wanderings. Climbing a particularly steep street, I noticed a familiar burning sensation in my lungs, the kind of feeling I would get when I was daft enough to go for a jog in younger days. I had forgotten the altitude here is 2850 meters, that's about 9000 feet. No wonder I was huffing and puffing, lugging my bags up the hotel steps!

I found my way to the La Ronda area of old town, a restored sixteenth century street with a long history as a hangout for artists and poets. I love to read menus and was looking for a place to bring Janice tomorrow when I stumbled into Al Negra Mala restaurant, drawn by its charming exterior that could have been a copy of a house in Seville or Granada in Spain.

A fountain played in the cobbled courtyard and narrow stairs lined with hanging plants opened out onto a charming upstairs dining area with tables overlooking the narrow pedestrian walking street.

"Hola! Could I see a menu please?" I asked the smiling lady who came to help me.

"Of course. Please sit down. Let me know how I can serve you."

I am writing in English, but actually we had to talk in Spanish, as she spoke not a word of our Mother tongue. Woe betide any independent traveler who attempts to navigate South America without pretty decent Spanish. Very few people outside hotels speak any English. I said a silent 'thank you' to my high school Spanish teacher who whipped my grammar into decent shape in just two years back in Cambridge, England.

The menu proudly recommended roast guinea pig as a national specialty and the fresh pan-fried sea bass. It all sounded exotic and enticing. As I scanned the pages further, an item in the drinks section caught my attention.

Chocolate with cheese.

Chocolate with cheese? What on earth was that?

I beckoned the smiling lady over and asked how this was prepared.

"Well, first you heat the milk. Then you add.... you know what, just follow me into the kitchen. We are not busy tonight and I will show you myself. It's on the house. My name is Victoria, like the queen of England. I am the owner here."

What a lovely invitation!

I walked over to her spotless kitchen and watched as she boiled some milk, then added some special chocolate chunks, together with some cinnamon to produce the desired flavor. She fished in the drawer for a special wooden stick with slits in and started to rub it vigorously between her hands, whipping and mixing the concoction into a chocolaty froth.

Finally it was mixed to her satisfaction. She proudly presented me with a cup of this steaming hot chocolate and next to the drink she placed a slab of very light local white cheese.
"You can dip the cheese in the drink or just eat it," explained my new friend, Victoria.

Yummy! It tasted delicious! I felt so touched by her kindness and wanted to know more about her. We had a lovely chat in my faltering Spanish and she told me she has run this restaurant for ten years and her whole family works there. Her daughter helps with the cooking in the kitchen and her husband waits tables. I thanked her profusely and promised to return with my friend and try her roasted guinea pig the next day!

****

Janice had finally shown up at 3:00 a.m. The next morning when I woke up, anxious to see if she had really arrived, I knocked on her door and there she was!

"Boy, am I happy you made it! What a journey! Thank God you got in last night!"

"It was touch and go again with the weather, but this time the fog was not too bad and the plane landed first try. I am SO happy to be here!"

Janice is my ideal traveling companion. She has a sunny disposition and is the kind of person who doesn't make a fuss about anything and goes with the flow, yet also will speak her mind when she needs to. She is athletic with a teenager's body despite being in her late fifties and I knew we would both enjoy lots of walking and outdoor activities together. She had spent the last few months volunteering in Guatemala working with a library program for children.

"I learned I am not cut out for third world volunteering," she said, when I asked her about her experience there. "It was pretty rough living in the jungle and I'm really happy to be back in civilization!"

We caught up more over breakfast. Bernice had laid out a scrumptious breakfast of real Swiss muesli and whole-meal bread with local cheese. We helped ourselves to delicious locally-grown coffee and tucked in. It was like having breakfast at Grandma's house. Everything a little old-fashioned and cozy, as we sat at the dining table that seated about six people.

A handsome young blond man came down from an upstairs room.

"Hi. Do you mind if I join you?" he asked politely, although I don't know where else he would have sat except on the kitchen counter. We exchanged the usual traveler

222

formalities and discovered his name was Stefan and he was from Finland. He led bird-watching tours all over the planet and had recently come back from Bhutan, a small mountain kingdom squished between India and China. It's the country where they measure gross national happiness.

"They really do seem to be happy people there," said Stefan "and the scenery is gorgeous. It's a country stuck in time and so peaceful. You really should go soon before it changes."

Great. Now I want to go to Bhutan. This is what I love about smaller guest houses and hostels – you meet the kind of fascinating people who would find the Holiday Inn boring and end up having stimulating conversation over a piece of toast. We thanked Stefan for all his great recommendations and set off to explore the old city in earnest.

Of course we visited the obligatory churches and monasteries. But for me, travel magic is made by unexpected encounters with people, and Quito's local inhabitants did not disappoint.

The first thing we noticed in the main square was the large number of locals walking around hawking unusual items. One man sold coffee filters, another sold shoelaces of many colors. We saw lots of Indian ladies selling colorful clothes for dogs. Trotting faithfully behind them, their own pooches modeled the outfits. The odd thing was that these vendors didn't sell anything else. I had to wonder how much they sold at all. I mean who suddenly needs a shoelace, a dog coat or a coffee filter?

There were a number of disabled folks plying a trade on the sidewalks. One blind lady played beautiful flute. Another lady in a wheelchair with no arms or legs was making colorful woolen scarves with her mouth, bending over a contraption that allowed her to pass the wool through a spool. We stopped to watch and Janice bought a scarf. I chatted to the lady, whose name was Maria, and asked if she got sore bending over like that all day. "Oh yes," she said in Spanish. "My shoulders get really tight."

She had a brilliant smile and a vibrant spirit and I felt drawn to connect with her a little more.
"Would you like me to massage them for you?" I offered, hesitant. I didn't know if she would accept touch from a stranger but suspected she could certainly use it.

"Por favor, si!" She looked delighted.

I walked behind her and gently pressed the flesh around her shoulders. My Lord, she was tight as a drum barrel! But as I kneaded and cajoled, her muscles softened and I could feel a relief spreading through her body. I was grateful to be able to help so lovely a soul.

While I was massaging her, a young girl ran up.

"Is that your daughter?" I asked.

"Yes," she said, pride glowing in her eyes. "Her name is Alison and she is eleven years old."

"So do you have a husband?"

"Yes I do."

"Well ask him to massage your shoulders for you every night when you go home. You could really use this regularly."

We took the required pictures of us all and sauntered off, promising to stop by and say hello again next time we were in Quito.

After lunch we found ourselves near the beautifully restored Theater. It looked shut but someone told us there was another entrance, which we found on the side street. There was a guard sitting in a small anteroom.

"Hello. Is it possible to see inside the theater?' I asked, feeling doubtful. There were no other tourists around.

"Wait here," said the guard and disappeared inside.

Two minutes later, he returned with the theater manager. "These two ladies want to see inside," explained the guard.

"Where are you from?" The manager was short. My five

foot four frame towered over him. Dave would seem like a giant to them here!

"Canada and England. We are really curious to see inside," said Janice in her best Spanish.

"Follow me," said the manager and proceeded to lead us through the back door to the most lovely, intimate theater.

"Our theater holds about seven hundred people. We stage operas and musical performances. Tonight we have a Polish pianist."

The grand piano was already in place on stage. "You are invited to come, if you like."

What a lovely offer! Unfortunately it was going to be a gala night and quite posh. My jeans and hiking boots would have looked out of place and we had no warm, smart clothes. We gracefully declined, impressed with this man taking time to show us around, obviously proud of his theater.

Later that day we walked back over to La Ronda area for dinner at Victoria's restaurant. Tonight was Friday and there were a couple of guys on her balcony making beautiful music with that haunting Andean flute and a guitar, singing local songs. We chose a table by the window overlooking the narrow street, packed with revelers and tourists alike.

"Welcome, Julia! Is this your friend?" Victoria came out from the kitchen to greet us with her million- dollar smile.

"This is my friend Janice from Canada," I said. "I've told her all about your wonderful hot chocolate and lovely restaurant. We can't wait to try your food!"

Janice had the lamb stew and I ordered the sea bass in shrimp sauce – all delicious. Across from our table sat a very handsome young man all on his own. Now we couldn't have that! As he got his drink, I lifted my glass and said, "Salud!"

"Salud" he replied with a smile.

We started chatting and as he was so obviously wanting some company, we invited him to join our table.

His name was Gustavo and he was from Chile. He was taking a six-week trip on his own through Peru, Bolivia and now Ecuador alone. He was a philosophy student and twenty-seven years old. And, it turned out, he loved yoga! He told us he had suffered from depression and three months ago had started a yoga practice and it had completely turned him around. Now he felt terrific and eager to study more.

I love it when the Divine sends people across my path like this! We went on to have a lovely conversation about the kind of yoga I teach and what other avenues he could look to explore in his own studies. I promised to send him an e-copy of my books.

"Unfortunately, they are all in English! They have not yet been translated into other languages."

Gustavo was thrilled and we promised to stay in touch.

After dinner back on the street, we were accosted by a lovely young lady in national dress who said she was about to dance in a folkloric performance and invited us to come and watch.

Well OK then.

We followed her down the narrow cobbled street, by now packed full of street performers, musicians, couples hand in hand and groups of locals, and into a small entrance; down some steps then out into an amphitheater. We took our seats and waited for the performance to begin.

Now I have to tell you, I have seen quite a few ethnic dance performances around the world and frankly, most of them are a bit of a yawn after the first ten minutes.

Not this one. This was hands-down the most lively, colorful, enthusiastic and shocking dance I have ever seen in my life! I was riveted!

It started with about thirty dancers leaping on the stage yelling and hollering, each of the ladies with different colored shawls that they twirled and hurled around. Their enthusiasm was contagious and I found myself clapping along with the bouncy music.

They left the stage and the music turned angry. A dirty-looking shaman, all hair and wearing black, pounced onto the stage. He cavorted around to the rhythm, hair swirling, completely covering his face. Then three maidens entered, obviously intrigued with this mass of male hormones. They tried to touch him, but he pushed them away. They tried to look under his cape, but he moved away. All this female attention must have had some effect, because all of a sudden, to everyone's surprise, he whipped out a four feet long penis and started to chase the maidens around the stage!

(No, not a real one, silly! It was made of felt!)

Off they all ran into the wings, but all this activity must have excited the locals. The next thing you know, three young men danced onto the stage followed by three young ladies. All of a sudden, the men jumped on top of the ladies and started to shag the living daylights out of them, everyone crying out in wild abandon! (Well they kept their clothes on, but you get the picture....).

Was this the x-rated folkloric version? I looked around the audience and mercifully there were no children asking Mommy and Daddy what those people were doing. It certainly made for a lively performance. Of course it ended with all us tourists being pulled up onto the stage to embarrass ourselves horribly trying to follow some basic dance steps. The locals were gracious and we all had a good time.

I got back to my seat and looked around for my little backpack. Gone. Maybe I had left it at the restaurant. We ran back and found Victoria. She hadn't found a thing. We all looked some more, but no backpack. Luckily, the only items inside were my Lonely Planet guidebook and a plastic cover-up for the rain. Victoria kindly ran upstairs and gave me a raincoat of her own! I thanked her profusely for her kindness and promised to return in two weeks and give it back. Tomorrow morning early we had a plane to catch. We were finally off to Galapagos!

Chapter 20

Dateline: February 4th, 2012
Galapagos

Sheets of rain greeted us as our plane landed at Baltra airport, the tiny Galapagos Island with an airstrip. I had chosen February for the trip because the water is warmer then and flowers bloom in the rain. The guidebooks all said the rain would be sporadic and brief. We hoped they were right!

Janice and I collected our bags and met Billy, our local guide and naturalist, at the arrivals hall. Billy is a local Ecuadorian with curly, black hair and speaks great English with a thick, gravelly accent, the kind that comes from smoking two packs of cigarettes a day for too many years. He told us to sit down and wait for the rest of the group that would join us on the boat.

First came Greg and Pat are a retired English couple from Norwich, which is near my hometown of Newmarket. They are keen ornithologists and Pat got the prize for having the biggest telephoto lens on her camera and the most photographic equipment.

I asked Greg how long they'd been married.

"Forty-six years. Could have done three murders for that," quipped the funny man.

God, I miss British humor!

Next to find us were live-wire thirty-somethings, Olwyn and Luke from London. Luke is a project manager in finance, currently taking a career break and his girlfriend, Olwyn, is her family firm's accountant. Despite the Welsh name, Olwyn is Irish with that lovely lilting accent. I felt pleased to have some London natives on board to catch up with news from my old hometown.

Two couples from Belgium and Sweden followed, along with a Mother and daughter from Holland.

Finally, a young, blonde, Dutch couple arrived touting two enormous suitcases plus two medium-sized bags... I wondered whatever they could need for an eight-day boat trip that was so important? Vivienne was five months pregnant. She was tall and wearing a clinging red and black woolen dress that would have looked too tight on a hooker, exposing her extended belly, plus black pumps and tights that would have been better suited to a dance hall. She looked hot and uncomfortable, her legs already swelling in the heat and humidity.

Patrick, her husband, was handsome but shorter then her, well muscled and with a determined look on his face. I wondered how he would manage to carry all those suitcases.

The group gathered, Billy packed us into a bus and we drove off across the island. The coastal area sported a barren landscape of lava rock and scrubby bushes, with tall prickly pear cactus trees standing like sentries guarding the land.

"These cactus trees are endemic to Galapagos," said Billy. "They are the only cactus species that grows like a tree. But watch out for their prickles or you will get a nasty cut!"

As we headed up into the hills, however, the landscape became lush and tropical, with more diversity in trees and vegetation. It also got noticeably cooler. We were headed to a private reserve where there was a good chance of seeing some giant tortoises.

"An adult can weigh as much as six hundred pounds," said Billy. "They, too, are a species that are unique to Galapagos and if we are lucky, we will see some today."

The sun came out and the rain stopped as we donned Wellington boots and walked the muddy trail of the tortoise reserve.

"Look Julia, there's one by that bush!" Janice whipped out her camera and got her first tortoise shot.

It's always exciting to see an animal in the wild for the first time and these tortoises really were huge and impressive. The animals in the reserve are free to come and go as they please but they like this area and can often be seen in large numbers eating grass and plodding slowly along by the meadows and ponds. We saw at least a dozen of the prehistoric-looking creatures and got very close for taking some great pictures. They did not seem to mind us at all.

When giant tortoises mate, they moo like a cow. It's the only vocalization they make. Billy had walked ahead on the trail and suddenly we heard him yelling at us.

"Come quickly! I can hear them mooing! They must be mating somewhere!"

Round the next corner, we saw them – a male standing on his hind feet mounting a female!

"It can last up to an hour!" said Billy, as we watched, fascinated, while the male tortoise humped himself silly on top of the female, breathing heavily as he hoisted that great weight up and down.

Back when whalers and sealers discovered these islands in the eighteenth century, the tortoise population was decimated from 400,000 to 10,000. Because the tortoises can survive for up to a year without food or water, they were coveted as a source of fresh meat on the long ship journeys home. Darwin even ate one. Now conservation efforts are bringing back their numbers with great success, all except for the sad plight of Lonesome George.

How would you feel if you were the last of your kind on the planet? Lonesome George was discovered all alone on the island of Pinta in the nineteen seventies. He is the last remaining tortoise from that particular island. Each tortoise has adapted a little differently to best suit the conditions on their home island and therefore George is a unique tortoise. He was brought to the Darwin breeding center on Santa Cruz Island and attempts have been made to breed him with other females from different islands. Unfortunately, efforts

231

have failed, as George does not seem particularly interested in sex.

One Swiss researcher even spent seven months with George, living in his enclosure and coating herself with the scent of females in heat, hoping to at least catch a drop of sperm from the lonely tortoise, but to no avail. All is not lost, however. Maybe he just hasn't met "the one" yet. He is only about seventy years old and could live another hundred years. There is still hope for his genetic line to continue, albeit as a crossbreed.

A visit to see this famous tortoise was next on our agenda, so we headed straight to the Darwin Research Center. There we saw one-year-old baby tortoises that are bred, then released back to the island of their origin. Introduced animals such as wild pigs and dogs and goats have been eradicated on some of these islands to give the tortoises a chance to survive. It seems to be working, as tortoise numbers are steadily increasing.

Naturally we had to visit Lonesome George. He is a bit of a reclusive personality and was hiding behind a rock during most of our visit. He must get completely fed up with all the fuss and bother over him, a simple tortoise trying to live a quiet life!

After our visit to the Darwin Center, Billy loaded us into dinghies at the dock and a couple of minutes later we were boarding "The Gran Poseidon", our home for the next eight days. It was surprisingly nice. Having been on boats before with cabins way too small to turn around in, let alone swing a cat, I was pleased that our cabin was a decent size and even had a closet! The bathroom was as big as mine at home with a real shower and flush toilet!

The entire boat was made from some exquisite Ecuadorian woods that gave the interior a classy yet cozy feel. Our beds were comfy and there was air-conditioning – luxury! And no wifi... at last I could disconnect completely from the outside world. No Facebook, no checking emails or phone messages... peace, quiet and nature – lovely!

That evening, Billy asked us all to come down for a

briefing on the next day's activities before dinner. He was playing guitar and passionately singing a lovely Spanish ballad when we arrived at the dining hall deck.

"I used to have a great voice, you know, but years of singing in smoky bars and drinking too much whiskey changed that," he said.

"Don't apologize," said Janice, ever the defender of musicians, being a folk-singer herself. "It's lovely to hear you play."

After our briefing, he asked the crew to come and introduce themselves. There were eight of them in total, including two gourmet chefs for our dining pleasure and a barman called Diego.

"I make the best capirinha in all of Galapagos!" he proudly proclaimed.

How could one refuse a challenge like that?

"I'll take one!" I said, eager to begin my celebration of this wonderful week. It was indeed excellent and helped whet my appetite for the delicious buffet meal about to be served.

I was excited to get to know thirteen interesting new people! On that first evening, Janice and I sat with Patrick and Vivienne. It turns out he is a concert and event organizer in Holland, handling big names like Madonna, Cold Play and summer festivals. He works eighteen to twenty-hour days regularly, so likes to come away to unwind and let his hair down.

Patrick is charismatic and high energy and I enjoyed his lively Dutch intelligence. He told me that he also used to be a Dutch ballroom dancing champion! Quite the over-achiever, that guy. I also noticed that while Janice and I tucked heartily into all the fresh vegetables on offer at the buffet, Patrick ate none.

"I just eat meat and potatoes," he said with a grin.

Vivienne sat quietly most of the time, smiling adoringly, but somehow illegible. That first night, I couldn't make out if she was his eye-candy who wouldn't interfere with the way he chose to live his life as long as he kept her in bling, babies and cruises, or his rock. Or both. In any case, she had snagged herself a handsome, wealthy entrepreneur and seemed pretty happy about it.

Once upon a time, when I was an impressionable London girl, I, too, could have made a choice to be a kept woman. There were offers. Yet I had chosen a different path in another country, one that came with challenges that gave me huge opportunities for growth. Looking at Vivienne that night, I felt doubly grateful for the choices I had made and the empowerment I feel today.

Exhausted from the long travel day, Janice and I were in bed by 9.30pm and slept like babies in our cozy cabin, waking only to hear the sound of the anchor being hauled back aboard. We sailed through the early hours, coming to anchor again about 4.00am.

****

We awoke to the sounds of gulls soaring overhead and sea lions barking... a gorgeous sunny morning, the 6.00am light surreal. We had sailed overnight to South Plaza Island and were anchored between it and North Plaza Island in a lovely sheltered bay. The boat's hardwood floors were perfect for early morning yoga before breakfast and it felt good to stretch out after all the traveling of yesterday.

"I smell sea lions!" announced Billy as he came down for his breakfast. "Get your good walking shoes, camera, water and sun cream and I'll see you at the dinghy station at 8:00 a.m."

Duly obedient, we gathered by the dinghies at the appointed time for our first foray onto National Park land. Vivienne, our pregnant Dutch princess, still had her dance shoes on together with a different tight-fitting dress. She and Patrick had not slept well and looked a little out of sorts. Their last vacation had been at an exclusive hotel in the Caribbean favored by movie stars. She'd packed for a five star cruise ship, not an intimate, casual boat trip with

234

hiking excursions on lava rock!

As we landed at the sea-lion colony, the strong smell of Galapagos perfume assaulted our nostrils... *guara* (seabird poop) mixed with sea lion urine. I almost stepped on an iguana! They were everywhere... land iguanas plus marine iguanas that swim in the sea. They eat the red sesuvium plants that look a bit like crimson ice plants. Tall prickly pear cactus trees dotted the otherwise barren landscape. Lava rocks glistened in the sun from years of sea-lion bodies rubbing them smooth. The contrast of green cactus trees, red sesuvium plants, and turquoise sea was startlingly beautiful.

"Oh my God!" Billy sounded excited. "So many sea lions! Be careful not to get too close to the large males. A sea lion bite will get infected and is a fast way to ruin your holiday."

He didn't have to tell me twice. The males make a loud barking sound and bare their teeth when they are defending their territory, which they did when we walked too close.

When they retired, Pat and Greg, the Norwich couple, had both taken up bird-watching as a hobby they could share and were really knowledgeable about the local birds. Ornithology and photography were now their focus for travel and have taken them around the world on a quest for great photographs of our feathered friends. They are also hilarious. The archetypal married-for-ever couple, she digs at him and he takes it all in his stride, giving it strongly back on occasion. They obviously adore each other.... and make a great team.

Pat saw a cactus finch land on a tree and start to probe its beak deep inside the yellow flower.

"That's a Darwin finch, you know. Darwin collected specimens from a few different islands and saw the slight variations in beak, each adapted to the particular flora of their own island. That's how he came to his 'Theory of Evolution'. Now where's Greg with my camera? He's always running off with it like I don't exist. Greg!"

Greg dutifully backtracked to find his wife, good-natured as ever.

■■■

We walked on to the cliff tops and saw giant frigate birds circling above us, gulls with bright red eyes (swallow-tailed gull) and red-billed tropicbirds, which are sleek, white gulls with long, wispy tails. The island was small and narrow and I could see the wisdom in limiting the number of tourists on this fragile ecosystem. We were only three groups that morning on the whole island... about sixteen people in each... and that was plenty.

The Ecuadorian government declared most of the Galapagos Islands a national park in 1959 and UNESCO has made it a World Heritage Site. Conservation efforts have been made to return the islands as much as possible to their natural state, restoring habitats, culling imported pests like the black rat or wild donkeys and limiting the amount of human impact on these precious islands.

Something else was evident; a peacefulness on the island, bereft of electro-magnetic frequencies, microwaves and other invisible pollutants of our modern world. The air itself felt at peace, soothing to the soul, with a calming effect on the mind, I felt privileged to be here in this pristine place, so far from crowds and the rest of civilization.

While we were walking, I took the opportunity to chat to Billy.

"How many months a year do you travel with groups, Billy?"

"About four to five," he replied.

"And what do you like most about your job?"

"I like meeting the people, and for me it's a rest and I get to play my guitar and read and snorkel and have fun."

"Well, can't you do that at home?"

"No, because at home I watch a lot of television and then I go to the bar and have drinks with my friends and I don't read. I play football a lot too.

"Do you have a wife?"

"No. I'm too old and ugly and I have no money."

I am not sure if this was meant as tongue in cheek because Billy was a good-looking man in my estimation; and only fifty-one, which is by no means OLD!

"So do you see yourself living here the rest of your life?"

"Yes, why not? I have my own house. I have my friends here. I like it. I go to the mainland once a year to visit my Mother. You know, when I was growing up, we were very poor and did not have enough to eat. My stepfather would drink all day and my Mother had to do laundry to feed us kids. When I was twenty-five, a friend suggested I go to Galapagos where people were making good money. I had to study very hard and learn English and very few people passed the test to be a naturalist guide. It took me a year, but I did it! In those days most guides were foreigners and I was one of the only Ecuadorian guides. Since then I have supported my Mother. She left her husband and has a good life now."

How admirable. What a reminder of how privileged we are, if we were lucky enough to come from a family where there was always enough food on the table. Billy told me, too, that he still dreamed of finding the right woman and even being a Dad. I wish him well.

We sailed the two hours to Santa Fe Island, our next destination, and anchored in a quiet bay. The turquoise water in the lagoon looked inviting.

"Get your snorkeling gear on – we are going to play with the sea lions!" Billy was enthusiastic for this next piece of our wildlife experience.

Sure enough, just at the entrance of the lagoon, there was a little surf break and a whole bunch of sea lions were surfing the waves, having the best time playing together and even chasing other fish that swam away, annoyed. The

237

juveniles were curious about us, circling and brushing by, liquid brown eyes imploring us to join them.

I had a flashback to my experience a year ago in Mexico.... here I was at last, having dreamed the dream, made my bucket list and acted on that initial inspiration. This time, the water was refreshing, not freezing, and we could stay in for an hour or so without feeling too cold.

In the lagoon, spotted eagle rays swam by. Luke saw a giant pacific green turtle swimming and called us all over. It glided gracefully around, front flippers like angels wings.

Back on the boat there were snacks waiting for us - hot chocolate, chicken wings and yucca bread. Hungrily, I devoured the snacks. Three meals a day and two snack-times, still I was hungry for every meal, metabolism fired up by all the swimming and stimulation.

Later, we went for an afternoon stroll from the beach to the cliffs. The sand was scratchy on my feet as I walked to the rocks to put on my shoes. The sea lions were sprinkled all over the beach and were fascinating in their behaviors. They did not seem to care at all that we were there. One baby even came up to Janice and gave her a seal kiss!

Have you ever been to a party where no-one was particularly interested in what you had to say, so you just kept moving on from group to group, feeling rejected? Well that's how one young sea lion must have felt on the beach. He moved from basking group to group and each time he laid down next to another sea lion, it would bark angrily and push him away. We never did see him snuggling happily with others of his kind.

****

The next morning, Christine, the young Dutch woman, found me on the deck doing my yoga practice and I invited her to join me.

"Oh I'm so stiff!" She remarked as she tried to ease her body into a position that for me would have been nothing.

"And that's why we do yoga!" I tried to encourage her.

238

"It will loosen you up and help you let go of all the tension in your body. You'll feel so much better."

"I did a class one time and felt like crying afterwards."

"Yes that happens a lot. We release the issues in our tissues. If it was sadness and grief that was the issue we will often want to cry it out. No need to analyze it – just allow it."

I hoped she would continue with a practice. Remembering Barbara's words in Bali that how we are at sixty begins at thirty, it would serve Christine well to start focusing more on her own body.

We had been sailing north all night. It had been a full moon and glassy calm water. In the morning, our guide Billy could hardly contain his excitement as we came down for our briefing.

"Today we are very fortunate. We are going to land in Genovese. I have been a guide for twenty years and have not been here for three years... the government has just allowed tour boats to come back here this week. And I smell hammerhead sharks today!"

On deck earlier, I had seen that we were anchored in the middle of a caldera, the top of an old volcano. It made a horseshoe shape with a small entrance for boats to enter and the island was small enough that anyone could walk the entire curved semi-circle in about an hour. After breakfast, we piled into dinghies and landed on the one small beach. It felt like we had arrived in Birdland and were invisible observers on their planet. The sound of birds was almost deafening... and boobies were everywhere!

NO! NO! NO! Not those kinds of boobies! This wasn't St Tropez in summer!

Billy had explained that Genovese is the only island in the world where you can see three kinds of booby birds... red footed, blue footed and nasca boobies. Now a booby is a strange looking bird. It's about the size of a large duck and has webbed feet and a long, pointy beak suited for spearing fish. It also makes one hell of a racket, especially

239

when courting! The male of the species will squawk and cry plaintively for hours on end in the attempt to attract a female mate during the two-week annual breeding season. If a female does not come, he continues until he gets hoarse and eventually loses his voice. It's a sad sight to see a lonesome male booby squawking away with only a peep coming out of his mouth, knowing that he has to wait another full year to find a mate again.

The super-cool thing about a booby is that it has designer feet. Bright blue ones and a blue-gray beak or bright red ones and a blue beak. The nasca ones are a little different, having black and white plumage, a bright orange beak and blue-gray feet. All of them are fascinating. We watched as the mating couples courted each other with beak kisses, preening, singing, presenting twigs to each other for the nest like a gift and eventually hopping on for a bird-shag. I know some men who could learn a thing or too from these boobies. They ignored us completely, almost as though they did not see us! Although one baby bird opened its mouth very wide and got very excited when I peered into it's nest in the vain hope that I might regurgitate my breakfast for it's dining enjoyment.

Frigate birds were there in large numbers too, circling overhead and nesting on branches. They have what looks like loose red scrotum hanging under their chins. When they are mating, the red scrotum blows up like a balloon to attract the female... completely irresistible if you are a female frigate bird.

I almost tripped over a brown heron, so well camouflaged was he against the rocks. These birds just do not have fear programmed into their genes. I asked Billy why the sailors of old didn't just pick them up and eat them. "They did eat them, but luckily for these birds, they don't taste too good. The tortoises did, which is why they came so close to extinction."

After our hike, we donned wetsuits and snorkels and took a swim by the cliffs. I saw lots of colorful fish but Janice hit jackpot and saw the hammerhead shark! Billy was right again – they were there but not all of us were lucky enough to see them. Still, any swim is invigorating and I love any opportunity to be in the water.

In the dinghy, Billy told us about the time, he was heading to Genovese a few years ago and never made it. The assistant captain never woke the proper captain up as they neared the rocks and the less experienced skipper smashed the boat into the rocks in stormy weather at 2.00am. Billy's group was all-Australian. They didn't panic, but as the alarm sounded, they grabbed their passports and headed for the lifeboat. It took a while for the boat to sink, but it was not recoverable. A navy boat rescued everyone and took them back to Santa Cruz, no real harm done. Hearing that, I was glad for our calm seas and great captain. We had had smooth sailing all the way, no *Dramamine* necessary for even my weak stomach.

Over dinner that night, I had a great conversation with Olwyn and Luke. Both live in London and have the art of conversation down. We put the world to rights, discussing politics, health care, Benny Hill and entertainment. I realized how much I missed this kind of intelligent and informed talk. As a London girl who grew up on the six-hour intimate dinner party scene, I was hungry for this type of engaged, vibrant conversation.

What I can say categorically is that the English are raised in a pub culture where we actually talk to each other over a pint. I believe this trains us to be more socially adept and perhaps to have greater conversational skills than in other cultures where there are fewer gathering places that foster conversation. Of course, it also trains us to drink like fishes, which comes with its own set of issues, but at least the average Brit can hold his own in any good discussion and most will have an informed opinion.

****

It's not every morning you wake up and say to yourself, "I'd think I'd like to go swimming with sharks today." However, that thought was exactly in my head as I wolfed down yet another delicious breakfast and added the

241

necessary calories for swimming in cool water. Besides I had missed the hammerheads yesterday and wanted my own shark experience.

Billy came down for his morning briefing and announced, "I smell sharks! We are going to be snorkeling by Daphne Island and there will be lots to see – maybe sea turtles, rays and white-tip reef sharks. But do not worry – they only eat French people!"

I have to say, as a tour guide myself, I know how hard it is to keep the group energy high each day, but Billy had been great with us. Every day he was enthusiastic about what we would see and genuinely excited to show us the natural wonders of his islands. His English vocabulary was excellent and the way he said, "baby" made me chuckle... it sounded more like "*boiby*". And of course there were lots of *boiby* birds, *boiby* sea lions and *boiby* iguanas to show us.

After breakfast, we gathered on the lower decks, snorkel gear at the ready. The first thing I saw as I jumped into the clear blue water was a huge tiger shark! Luckily it was about thirty feet below me, swimming quickly away in the opposite direction. Although Billy had told us that the sharks here were fairly harmless and would not bother us, (and I have no French blood in my body!) the sight of so large a fish right below me still had my heart racing!

Brown speckled starfish were plastered onto rocks like rubber stamps, mandala patterns of orange design on their chubby, five-pointed bodies. Turtles weaved their way gracefully through the water and schools of fish danced their choreographed underwater ballet. There was no coral here, (the water's too cold except in El Nino years), just rocks, but the sea life was plentiful enough to keep our interest for an hour. Shoals of large gray razor surgeon fish with yellow tails, sergeant majors, parrot fish, grunts, blue and gray morasses, even a golden tiger eel, covered with brown spots.

Later that day, as we rested on a lovely sandy beach, I saw Billy withdraw to the shade of a tree and immerse

242

himself in a Natural History book. Good for him, keeping up on his education. The sun was strong and I applied factor-thirty sunscreen all over and threw a shirt over my face. Except for fair-skinned Olwyn, I saw the younger European girls basking in full sun, including their faces, something I would never dream of doing now in my older years.

But Paradise can have its drawbacks.

"Ow," yelled Janice as a huge horse fly tried to take a bite out of her leg. The regular flies were bothersome too and some people were getting bitten by mosquitoes. It didn't take long for Pat and Greg to get fed up with the beach. Greg's ankles were turning a brighter red by the minute and Pat's shoulders were burning, their fair English skin not tolerating the equatorial sun. I think we were all happy to leave the beach and get back to the boat that day.

At his 6:30 p.m. briefing Billy announced:

"Tomorrow we are losing some of our group. The people who took the five-day cruise will be taken back to Baltra for the airport. I am so sad. You are my best group ever."

We all laughed, assuming he said that to every group. But it actually really had been a good group with interesting people, a lot of commonality.

"We will be collecting new guests. Unfortunately they are from Ecuador and Spain. I have to tell you, in my twenty years of experience as a guide, my own country people have always been the worst kind of guests. They are easily bored and after a couple of days are asking, 'Where is the discotheque? Where can I buy lobster?' The Spanish are nearly as bad."

"Well maybe these people will be absolutely wonderful," said Janice, optimistic and cheery as usual.

We would all find out soon enough. Janice I decided to be the official welcoming committee for the new group so we would go with Billy to the airport the next day... plus we wanted to check email   with wifi at the airport!

243

That night, our group was in the mood for celebration! Janice broke out her guitar before dinner and enchanted everyone with her lovely singing. She writes her own tunes and also does Canadian classic folk songs. Everyone loved her and it set the tone for a happy dinnertime. It was one of those lovely moments when somehow the whole shebang came together.... the right place, people and moment; for me, pure ecstasy. I felt uplifted, relaxed and full from all the nature we had seen.

The bar soon ran out of gin and red wine. We went to the upper deck and Greg, fine Englishman that he is, broke out his cigar stash to share. Everyone pledged to stay in touch and share photos.

By 9:00 p.m., Janice and I were exhausted and went to bed, leaving the younger crowd to party on.

****

The others partied hard on the upper deck till late. As I got up at 6:00 a.m. to do my yoga practice, I saw the evidence – empty bottles and full ashtrays everywhere. Patrick emerged at breakfast hung over and feeling sick. Vivienne had gotten bitten badly by mosquitoes at the beach and was feeling off, too. Olwyn was also not feeling well. Maybe just as well we were having a morning off from wildlife spotting.

At the airport, we said our good-byes to the people leaving and greeted the new people... a lovely young couple from Spain called Jesus and Sonia, who were here to film a travel promo film for her travel agency; a Dutch guy called Stan with his Ecuadorian girlfriend, Valerie, who both worked in the aviation industry in Qatar; plus Yuko, a Japanese girl of twenty-eight from Tokyo traveling alone.

Once all settled back on board, we sailed through the night and woke the next morning to a very interesting sight – an island the shape of a hat lay to our west and a bleak volcanic land mass straight ahead. The volcanic eruptions had left a fascinating landscape and I couldn't wait to explore it!

"Good morning everybody!" Billy was particularly upbeat today. "The sun in shining and we are going to have a beautiful day. And I am smelling manta rays!"

I love volcanic islands and felt totally excited about both our upcoming hike and swim! The early morning light was lovely as we disembarked onto the small, sandy beach, once again covered with sea lions and crabs, Sally-lightfoot crabs to be exact, red as a blood orange, with bright blue chins.

Billy explained that an ancient sailor had been entranced by a dancing girl on a Caribbean island whose name was Sally. She was light on her feet. These crabs scamper across rocks and dance with each other, so he named them Sally-lightfoot crabs. They are the only crabs in the world that shed their shells like a snake, crawling under a rock on land for a week to allow the new one to grow undisturbed.

When the male wants to mate, he will start to froth at the mouth, then does his little crab dance with the female, jumps on her for a few minutes, runs away to a tide-pool then repeats the same process again a couple more times. When he is finished, they separate and the female runs away from him as fast as she can while the male chases after her. If he catches her, he will eat her! To fool him, she will drop a leg so he can munch on that and let her get away. That's how you can spot the crabs that are not virgins – they have less than their usual five legs each side!

These crabs are scavengers. They will eat a dead seal, seal excrement, bird poop, anything really. If you were to get drunk and pass out on a beach here, you would awake covered in crabs nibbling away at you!

After our hike we went for one of the most memorable snorkeling trips of my life, for two reasons. The first came right after we had all jumped in the channel that lies between Chinese Hat and Santiago Island. Billy started screaming at us to swim towards him and sure enough, headed our way was the biggest manta ray I have ever seen! At least ten feet across, it glided elegantly through the

245

calm, turquoise waters of the channel slowly enough for us to follow it for a few minutes. It was magnificent! I felt blessed to have set my eyes on so graceful a creature.

The other surprising highlight were the charcoal-gray marine iguanas that swam beside us near the rocks. Their prehistoric faces peered out above the water looking menacing. Four feet paddling and tail a swishing, they looked strangely out of place underwater until they clambered out on to the rocks to feed on the algae. Their sharp, silver nails looked like they were fresh out of the salon, all long and perfect, and went 'clack' as they clawed the rocks. Perfectly camouflaged, they were the same color as the lava and it took a while for my eyes to adjust before I could see how many were actually resting on the rocks.

All that hiking and swimming made me hungry!

The food on the boat had been very fresh, varied and plentiful. But the desserts were, well, let's say interesting. That night, we were served a "sweet tomato," an Ecuadorian specialty dessert. Apparently this is called a "tree tomato" and although it looks like a tomato it is, in fact, a fruit. The locals boil it in its own juice with some sugar and voila! ...a disgusting-tasting dessert that we thought was meant to be a joke on the tourists!

One spoonful was enough for me. It tasted like sour wallpaper paste!

"Who wants another dessert?" I asked, never expecting anyone to raise their hand.

"I will," said Luke!

Olwyn raised her eyebrows. "That man eats absolutely anything."

Sure enough, Luke tucked in and soon downed his second helping. The rest of us watched with some amazement.

****

That stormy night, the water was rougher and the boat rocked like crazy. Although I slept well after so long in the water, most of the guests did not. Janice doused herself with *Dramamine* like it was going out of fashion. To make matter worse, the water pump to the upstairs rooms had failed during the night.

I saw Pat storming up the stairs as I was doing my morning yoga. "Don't anyone else tell me it's a beautiful morning or I'll kill them!" she exclaimed in the very uptight, constrained way that British people do when they are annoyed. It was a lovely sunny morning so I wondered what was up.

Her toilet had not flushed well all week. In the middle of the night, with a stomach upset, poor Pat got up when the boat was rocking like crazy, staggered to the toilet to do her business then had to use the plunger that they had given her to get it down. That was even OK. The last straw was when she couldn't wash her hands afterwards! She felt so dirty.

"Billy, I want a word with you," I heard her say over breakfast.

I smiled inwardly as I watched Billy's expression change to one of alarm in the face of Pat's evident wrath! He was actually very compassionate and kind to her and went to speak to the ship's engineer to see what could be done.

Back with the group, Billy announced, "I smell penguins!" with a grin. Sure enough, on the dinghy ride over to Isabela Island, we saw a penguin standing on the rocks and another one swimming right by our boat! Pat was overjoyed... it was the only other bird she had really wanted to see.

We went on a tour of the island by open bus, driving through lovely mangrove forests, stopping when giant tortoises or iguanas crossed the road in front of us. The tour culminated at the "wall of tears".

In 1946, prisoners from the main land were brought here to serve out their terms. The guards entrusted to watch over

247

them were harsh, cruel and unregulated. They forced them to build a wall of lava, for no reason other than to keep them busy. It's huge. Maybe eight feet thick and runs two hundred meters long. If a prisoner were unruly, they would make him stand naked in the hot sun all day with out moving. If he moved, he was shot.

The prisoners had a saying, "The weak die and the strong cry." Now the wall is part of a park that can be visited and stands as a monument of man's inhumanity to man. It made me shudder to think of all the men who died here in horrendous circumstances. I made my own personal prayers for them.

We walked slowly back into town and the Dutch contingent and partners all headed to the bar for beer. Next thing I heard was they were going to eat lunch there, as they could get steak and lobster. Patrick ate two steaks, with no vegetables of course. The Ecuadorian girl, too, ordered lobster just as Billy had predicted and went back early to the boat, completely disinterested in more wildlife viewing, missing the fascinating walk we had through the mangroves and flamingo lagoon.

The last day we were all packed and ready by 7:00 a.m. - all except Patrick and Vivienne, that is. As I walked past their cabin, I saw clothes strewn all over the floor. They were nowhere near ready. Not only that, but they had run up a $400 bar bill and had no cash to pay it! A crew member had to run Patrick into town to get money from the ATM while we all waited.

"I could have told you this would happen," Pat whispered in my ear. "His sort are all mouth and no substance. Well, I'm not lending him any money."

Half an hour later, Patrick returned, pockets stuffed with cash ready to settle his debts. Still, the rest of us were not impressed. There was a plane to catch and everyone had to wait.

Eventually we all landed on the dock and said our goodbyes. Janice and I were staying another week in Puerto Ayora, the main tourist town on the islands, to dive and

248

relax. The rest were all flying straight back to the mainland. I was sad to see our friends move on, but hoped to stay connected and see them again soon, maybe at a reunion in London.

Afterthought

It has been an amazing week, one I will never forget.

Being with Olwyn and Luke I saw my younger self, the kind of person I was when I was living in London; disillusioned with the glitz and glamour of the city yet unsure where to go next, which path to tread in life. I could easily have chosen to stay in England if fate had not intervened, possibly ending up living in the countryside like Greg and Pat, content yet somewhat bored.

I still have the English girl in me - she's part of my fabric. But when I turned left at the big white pig, I ended up leaving my country to become someone else. I became a woman capable of expanding my senses, exploring the mystical and going beyond the restrictions of my upbringing.

I see my own evolution now. I have become a hybrid creature, a cross between sophisticated London girl and California mystic, comfortable in these two different worlds yet sticking out like a sore thumb in both. A misfit. Yet that too has its gifts. I have become my own person, no longer needing or seeking approval from either society.

And there is power in that. Disconnecting from the need to be a certain way has helped me to find MYSELF. I have learned to follow my own dreams, including those which led me here to Galapagos, to this magnificent land that time almost forgot. I feel my own freedom, freedom to express who I am and to follow my heart.

The animals we saw here in Galapagos had no fear in their programming.

Observing this behavior invites me to ask, "Who am I without my fear? What more could I accomplish? What would I do if fear no longer stood in my way?" I will ponder these questions in the months to come, to see where my life could go if I let go of more of my own fear.

As I sit on the beach here in Santa Cruz Island writing

250

this, a Darwin finch has landed on my red backpack and is pecking away at the banana skin that sits exposed in the bag. I could reach out and grab him.

But I won't.

He warbles away merrily and blesses me with his sweet finch song.

My heart leads me home again now; home to Dave, my loving man waiting for me with open arms and kindred soul. We are excited to merge our dreams, to share new, co-created desires that we will manifest together. Maybe we will teach, maybe we will write together. I don't know yet. I only know that however we move forward, it will be in authenticity and truth for both of us, sharing our light and our love in the service to all who cross our path. I look forward to that with a happy heart and a lightness of spirit as I warble my own unique song to the world.

About Julia Tindall…

Julia Tindall is a yoga and tantra teacher based in Sacramento, California. She leads yoga workshops at Harbin Hot Springs and other power spots in Northern California and escorts groups on yoga vacations to Mexico, Costa Rica, Hawaii, Bali and Thailand.

Julia is the author two books on *jnana* yoga, the art of self-inquiry – "20 Questions for Enlightened Living, Peace and Freedom through Jnana Yoga" and "Your Presence is Enough." Both books are available by mail order on Julia's website or from www.amazon.com. Julia's *jnana* yoga group is still ongoing in Sacramento.

For more information on Julia and her retreats, plus pictures that illustrate this book, go to www.juliatindall.com and www.Leftatthebigwhitepig.com.

Made in United States
Troutdale, OR
02/25/2024

17960160R00146